Caring Across Cultures

Preparing for Effective Misssionary Nursing

Grace Tazelaar, MS, RN

NCF
PRESS

NCF Press
A ministry of Nurses Christian Fellowship®
of InterVarsity Christian Fellowship®/USA
P.O. Box 7895, Madison, WI 53707-7895
World Wide Web: www.ncf-jcn.org
E-mail: ncf@ivcf.org

NCF Press is the book-publishing division of Nurses Christian Fellowship®
of InterVarsity Christian Fellowship/USA®. In response to God's love, grace and truth:
the purpose of Nurses Christian Fellowship, as a ministry of InterVarsity Christian
Fellowship/USA, is to establish and advance in nursing, within education and practice,
witnessing communities of nursing students and nurses who follow Jesus as Savior and Lord:
growing in love — for God, God's Word, God's people of every ethnicity and culture, and
God's purposes in the world. NCF is a member movement of Nurses Christian Fellowship
International. For information about local and regional activities, contact NCF at the address
above or by e-mail at ncf@ivcf.org or through our website, www.ncf-jcn.org.

Cover photograph: Jim Whitmer

ISBN: 0-9723123-6-6

Table of Contents

Preface

While I was in college, a friend encouraged
me to select a life verse. After prayer and
Bible study, the Lord led me to Psalm 73:28.
*"But for me it is good to be near God; I have made
the Lord GOD my refuge, to tell of all your works."*

It has been my life's desire to grow closer to God so that I can share with others the great things he has done. My spiritual journey has allowed me to see God at work during twelve years of teaching nursing, six years as a missionary in Uganda, and seven years coordinating domestic health ministries while living in Mississippi.

When I joined the advisory board for Global Health Outreach, the short-term mission organization that is part of the Christian Medical and Dental Association, as a representative of Nurses Christian Fellowship, Dr. Sam Molind, the executive director, asked me to arrange for continuing nursing education credit for nurses going on mission projects. Prior to leaving for Uganda, I had benefited from a mission board that prepared me well for my work overseas. I was and remain grateful for that preparation. I had also observed other missionaries who were not prepared for the challenges that a mission experience provides. I grieved for and with them as they struggled to make sense of their mission experience. With the encouragement of Mary Thompson, the national director of Nurses Christian Fellowship, I accepted Dr. Molind's challenge to develop a continuing nursing education module to prepare nurses for a mission experience.

The personal experiences used throughout the text are included to illustrate God's great work in my life and should not be construed as a desire to draw attention to myself. God has redeemed many situations and many of my failures. I share them to give him the glory and the honor for what God has done. I wrote this program with a prayer that others might be well prepared to grow closer to God through a mission experience. Then they too can share with others the great things our Lord has done for them.

In addition to Mary Thompson and Dr. Molind, I am grateful to Melodee Yohe, who initially edited the text, Ruth Snapp, who provided her expertise on the continuing education program, and Judith Allen Shelly, the NCF resources director, for publishing it.

UNIT 1: JESUS AS A MISSIONARY

Objectives
At the end of this unit, you should be able to:
1. Identify principles for mission from the life of Jesus Christ
2. Develop a personal plan for mission, based on these principles

The diesel-fueled Land Rover pulled into the Terego archdeaconry training center around midday. I was excited about beginning the first training session of health workers in this area. My Ugandan colleague, Margaret Ejoga, a registered midwife who came from this region, would be teaching village women selected by their parishes to be community health workers (CHWs). CHWs are people who teach others in their community the lessons of health that they learned during the four days of training.

The training center consisted of mud and thatch houses, arranged in a square around a gazebo that served as our classroom. Each parish in the archdeaconry had built a home where the lay ministers from their parish could live while they studied there. We would stay in these lovely homes for our CHW training session. The archdeaconry had arranged for someone to cook for us. We brought food with us for the five days—twenty kilos of sugar, tea, a sack of enya flour (made from fermented cassava root, the local staple food), beans, tomatoes, onions and groundnuts. From her uncle, Margaret procured a sheep to be slaughtered for the closing meal. The women arrived throughout the afternoon. Most had to walk ten to twenty miles carrying bedding on their heads and babies on their backs.

The principal of the training center greeted us warmly, then informed us that there was a problem. There always seemed to be some sort of a problem for each of our sessions. This time the

borehole that supplied safe water for the center had broken. They
had been unable to repair it before we came. We expected about
twenty women for the training, plus visitors on
the final day, and the nearest source of safe water was five
kilometers down the road.

We collected all the available jerry cans (plastic containers
used to transport liquid commodities) and water containers and put
them in the back of the pick-up truck. Since I was the only driver,
several children went with me to direct me to the borehole. We
pumped water and filled the containers and returned to the training
center. This was repeated two or three times a day for five days. I
had learned only enough Lugbara, the local language, to greet and
make my needs known. Margaret taught the lessons in the vernacular.
Each night we went over the lessons together and then as she
taught, I went on water runs.

It was hot and tiring work to pump and carry water. I was
grateful that I didn't have to put it on my head and walk back the
five kilometers, as many women did. I have to admit that I wondered
why God had asked me to get a master's degree in nursing and
come to Uganda to drive a Land Rover to collect water for five days.

The answer came on the last day. Ugandans have learned from
the British to be very formal. The training sessions had to have a
closing ceremony to which local dignitaries from the government,
churches and clinics were invited. Food was always a part of the
celebration, and an invitation to a free meal was never turned
down. During the ceremony the women recounted for the visitors
all that they had learned. It was a joy to hear them tell about the
importance of latrines, washing hands prior to eating, safe drinking
water, and to describe how to make oral rehydration solution. They
sang and performed dramas about the lessons.

Then the thanksgiving began. The women thanked Margaret for her teaching, the parishes and archdeaconry for providing the means for them to come, the cooks for cooking and the visitors for coming. Then one woman got up and began to speak. Someone translated for me. "We want to thank Grace for coming. She is just like Jesus. She left the comfort of her home in America to be with us. She served us every day by collecting the water we needed for cooking, drinking and bathing. We did not have to worry about getting water the entire time we were here."

I felt humbled. I thought I had not been effective because I could barely speak Lugbara; I hadn't been able to teach about health or Jesus and had done nothing but fetch water the entire week. But the Holy Spirit used my service to speak of Jesus to the women who had sacrificially come to the training session.

Jesus lived among us

What can we learn about Christian mission from Jesus the Missionary? First, he left his home in heaven to become Immanuel, God with us. "Long ago God spoke to our ancestors in many and various ways by the prophets, but in these last days he has spoken to us by a Son, whom he appointed heir of all things, through whom he also created the worlds. He is the reflection of God's glory and the exact imprint of God's very being, and he sustains all things by his powerful word. When he had made purification for sins, he sat down at the right hand of the Majesty on high" (Heb 1:1-3). Jesus left the splendor of heaven to join this sinful world. Sometimes God calls us to leave the comfort of our homes to join others who do not have running water, electricity and indoor plumbing. Whenever someone says to me, "You gave up so much to go to Uganda," I say it was a privilege. In fact, it is miniscule in comparison to what Jesus did for me.

Jesus served the poor

Not only did Jesus leave the comforts of heaven, but he came to one of the poorest places on earth. His parents were simple, unassuming, working-class people. They lived under a foreign-dominated government. They had to walk wherever they went. Jesus knew what hard work was. He experienced all of life as a human. He was tired, hungry and felt the pain of beating and crucifixion. He experienced the emotions of joy at wedding feasts, sorrow at the death of friends and anger at those who exploited the poor in the name of religion. Having never done anything wrong, he was unjustly accused and sentenced to death. When we go on a mission trip or leave our homes and families to live among people of lesser means; when we experience physical tiredness, when we hunger for a familiar food or have a bout of dysentery; when we share in the celebrations of our host cultures or mourn the death of malnourished children; when we are misunderstood culturally and live under foreign governments, we are doing nothing more than what Christ has done for us.

Jesus spent years in preparation

For thirty years before beginning his official ministry, Jesus lived and worked among the people he came to serve. He trained under his earthly father to become a carpenter. In my case, I taught in a school of nursing for twelve years before the Lord opened doors to Uganda. At one point, I thought that my calling was preparing nurses for the mission field rather than going myself. During these years, I gained valuable experience in nursing education, curriculum development, Bible study and ministry. When I finally got to Uganda, I was surprised that all these experiences were used to teach community health workers, write curricula for them and minister through the church. My relationship with God and my ability to trust him with my life was strengthened during the years prior to leaving home. My call to missions was refined, and my values for ministry were shaped while I was learning my role as a nurse educator. I was blessed with two nurse mentors, one an administrator and one a former missionary, who guided me in the early years of my career and modeled ministry. What may have seemed like a wilderness on the road to becoming a missionary nurse was really the foundation for future ministry as a missionary.

Jesus served a limited term

I spent six years in Uganda. That may seem like a long time, but for missionaries who have dedicated their entire lives to serving God in another culture, it is a short time. The first three years were in the north of the country, working with a diocesan health project; the final three years were in the capital, Kampala, developing the Primary Health Care (PHC) Department of the Ugandan Protestant Medical Bureau (UPMB). This agency represented Protestant health work to the Uganda Ministry of Health. For both assignments, my goal was to work myself out of a job.

Jesus' public ministry lasted approximately three years. He also worked himself out of a job by teaching and equipping disciples to carry on the work after his death and resurrection. He poured himself into a few people whom he felt could continue the work. The disciples were a motley crew, not necessarily people we would have selected as dynamic, potential leaders with charisma and influence.

Jesus worked himself out of a job

In Uganda, I was blessed with two excellent nurse colleagues, who continued the work after I left. All of us had strengths and potentials, but we also had our flaws and weaknesses. I focused on developing my colleagues' leadership and management skills, rather than conducting the project myself. Through them, many more have been reached than I could have ever done alone.

We need to make the best use of the time God has given us. Sometimes, for missionary nurses, that is translated into frantic activity—seeing as many patients in a day as we can, preaching the gospel message in the evenings and Sundays, getting funding for our projects, and micromanaging the laboratory, pharmacy, car pool and health education program. I find it interesting that Jesus never seemed to be hassled. He didn't find it necessary to heal every sick person in the region, or to teach and preach in every synagogue, or to worry about where he would spend the night and get his next meal.

Jesus restored *shalom*

Jesus cared not only for the physical needs of the sick he encountered, he provided for their total healing. He restored their health, their *shalom*. He reconciled them to God, to themselves and to others, as well as caring for their physical ailments. He spent time alone with the Father to be spiritually refreshed. He accomplished his ministry through relationships, not frantic activity. He attended to matters at hand, while using these interruptions to teach his disciples about faith, servant leadership and the kingdom of God. This is a good model for our ministry.

Jesus withdrew to allow his followers to flourish

Saying goodbye to Margaret after three years left me struggling. Could I trust that she would figure out how to continue the health program? I wasn't sure that I had laid an adequate foundation for the PHC department. Would it continue to function smoothly when I left the country? I took comfort in the fact that Jesus ascended to heaven before the disciples began the church. He knew that if the church was to grow and flourish, it would require the work of the

Holy Spirit to direct it, and for the Holy Spirit to come, he needed
to return to the Father. The Lord gave me peace about leaving the
work to my colleagues when it was time to leave. For my colleagues
to grow into their leadership positions, I needed to get out of the way.

Missionaries must think about how and when to turn over
ministry to local brothers and sisters in Christ. Leaving too soon
doesn't provide the base necessary for continuing the ministry.
However, staying too long can lead to dependency. Sometimes
missionaries must leave when the government tells them that they
are no longer welcome. As missionaries, we must be cognizant that
our time is limited. We may never see the results of our efforts.

Jesus trusted the Father

Before his death and resurrection, Jesus prayed for his followers,
entrusting them and their ministry to the Father (Jn 17). While
we serve as missionaries, the Lord will grow our faith to expect
that the seeds we plant will be watered and nurtured through the
provision of the Holy Spirit. The work is the Lord's, not ours. He
will bring about its completion. We depart, praying along with
Paul, the first missionary, "Constantly praying with joy in every one
of my prayers for all of you, because of your sharing in the gospel
from the first day until now. I am confident of this, that the one
who began a good work among you will bring it to completion
by the day of Jesus Christ" (Phil 1:4-6).

Suggested Activities:

1. Review the life of Christ in the Gospel of Luke, listing the principles Jesus demonstrated in his ministry.

2. Use these principles to formulate a model of mission for yourself. Consider such things as:

    • In what ways can you learn to understand and identify with the people you hope to serve?

    • How will you serve the poor in your ministry?

    • In what ways are you doing that now?

    • Review your education and experience to this point.

    • In what ways has it prepared you for mission?

    • What further preparation do you need?

    • How long will you stay?

    • What is your plan for working yourself out of your present ministry involvements?

    • Think about what it might mean to restore *shalom* in the context of the culture you will be entering.

    • Develop a long-range plan for training others to replace you in your new ministry. How can you avoid creating dependency?

    • Examine your present devotional life.

    • What needs to change? Determine practical ways to keep your relationship with the Lord strong while you are serving as a missionary.

UNIT 2: PREPARING SPIRITUALLY

Objectives
At the end of this unit, you should be able to:
1. Examine areas of spiritual growth to which a mission experience contributes
2. Explore the biblical basis for missions
3. Prepare a personal testimony that tells of *your* spiritual journey

I visited a nursing school friend who was a missionary in Uganda a year-and-a-half before I went there as a missionary. It was an exploratory trip. Could I live as a missionary? Was God calling me to be a missionary? Wasn't I already a missionary serving as a faculty advisor to the student chapter of Nurses Christian Fellowship? I returned from that trip thinking, "God, I could never live like that!" It wasn't so much the lack of running water and electricity. It wasn't the large insects and snakes that bothered me. It was the drunken boy soldiers with AK-47s at the roadblocks, the immigration and custom officials who looked for bribes and seemed to undress me with their eyes, and the memories of a talk by Helen Roseveare, a missionary doctor in the Congo who had been beaten and raped during the rebellion that frightened me. She had written Philippians 3:10-11 as an inscription in my book, "I want to know Christ and the power of his resurrection and the sharing of his sufferings by becoming like him in his death if somehow I may attain the resurrection from the dead." Was I willing to put my life on the line as Jesus had done for me? That was the question I needed to settle with God. Jesus said, "He called the crowd with his disciples, and said to them, 'If any want to become my followers, let them deny themselves and take up their cross and follow me. For those who want to save their life will lose it, and those who lose their life for my sake, and for the sake of the gospel, will save it. For what will it profit them to gain the whole world and forfeit their life?' " (Mk 8:34-36).

Mission is not so much about what we are doing for God but what God is doing in us through mission. By leaving our comfort zones in a mission experience, God is able to address the areas in our lives that need to be exposed for spiritual fine-tuning. We may not always be prepared for what is exposed. I always thought that I had committed my whole life to Jesus, but when confronted with the possibility that I could lose my life by living in a country torn by civil war, God was saying, "Are you wholly committed to me?" It was the first of many times God would challenge my idea of what it meant to serve him.

Dealing with injustice

Somehow I was led to believe that because I had left home to serve God, I could expect a blessing. This is one misconception perpetuated by Christians. If anything, life became more challenging. I saw numerous unexplainable injustices that caused me to question God's sovereignty and justice. A Ugandan church leader was killed in an ambush. A fellow missionary died in an auto accident. Christian women who were faithful to their husbands died of AIDS. Children suffered and died from malnutrition, malaria, measles and polio. I was often knocking on the doors of heaven, asking God, "Why?" The answer never came. But I had a greater sense of who God is and a greater appreciation for the price that Jesus paid to reconcile the world to himself. "In Christ God was reconciling the world to himself, not counting their trespasses against them, and entrusting the message of reconciliation to us" (2 Cor 5:19). Through the difficult times overseas, I learned more about who God is and my limited understanding of him grew to new heights.

Learning to trust

A growing trust in God to provide for everyday needs contributed to expanding my knowledge of him. After three months of no rain, the tanks on the house that collected and stored rainwater from the roof were nearly empty. It had become convenient to get water from the rain tank as opposed to going down the road a kilometer or so to the borehole. I prayed that God would send rain so that the tanks could once again be filled. That night we had our first rain of the season. I was so thankful. Safe water is abundant in the U. S. We take it for granted that when we turn on the tap water will come forth. Living without the comforts of life in the U. S. reminds us how much God has given to us. We don't always recognize that it is God who provides these comforts. The knowledge that God cares about these details in our lives and daily provides for them helped me to trust him for bigger matters.

When I returned home from Uganda, some people thought I must have taken leave of my senses. The first time I went to get gas in my car, I asked someone in the station, "Do you have petrol?" Insuring a supply of fuel had consumed a good deal of my time and energy in Uganda. I had moved to Mississippi where the rains are heavy at times. I was scheduled to travel about 40 miles during a rainstorm. I asked, "Will the road be passable?" Muddy roads and floods made travel hazardous in Uganda. Again, my friends looked at me curiously. Of course the road is passable; it was only raining. Every time we get in a vehicle, we assume that we will arrive at our destination safely. That was not true in Uganda. Travel required God's provision and protection. One trip of 300 miles included two punctured tires, three out of four engine mounts broken, one crossing of the Nile River on a ferry that was half under water, numerous encounters with drunken soldiers at roadblocks, two extra cans of diesel and two days of travel on rutted, muddy roads.

The sight of large animals in the game park and the coolness and darkness of driving through the rainforest tempered the challenge of the journey. I always knew that it was God who was our co-pilot on safari, and his angels were protecting us on our way.

The stories of travel on mission trips provide many great "adventure tour" sagas. They give us exciting tales of God's provision and protection. It often is the allure of these adventures that entices spirited health professionals to step out in faith on a short-term mission project. People return home to regale their Sunday-school classes and others with great stories of life as a missionary.

Evangelism

If we are serious about mission, however, we understand that there is more to the picture. Following Jesus' example, the purpose of Christian mission is to present the good news that God wants to have a personal relationship with us through Jesus. For those with the gift of evangelism, this is the heart of mission. "But how are they to call on one in whom they have not believed? And how are they to believe in one of whom they have never heard? And how are they to hear without someone to proclaim him? And how are they to proclaim him unless they are sent? As it is written, 'How beautiful are the feet of those who bring good news!'" (Rom 10:14-15).

Developing a heart for sharing the good news should begin before leaving on a mission trip. It begins with a study of the Bible to understand the big picture that God has for this world. In Genesis 3, after Adam and Eve have sinned, God seeks them out where they are hiding and provides clothing for their nakedness. Throughout Scripture we see that God seeks out the lost. Mission is his endeavor. The amazing thing is that he allows us to partner with him in this endeavor. The knowledge that it was God who seeks and saves sinners, and that it didn't depend on me was a

freeing truth. Regular time in the study of God's Word is essential
preparation for missions. InterVarsity has a Bible study guide on
missions to help one understand mission from God's perspective,
as outlined in the Bible.[1]

If I am God's partner in this endeavor, I need to be prepared to
tell others what God has done for me through Jesus Christ. Everyone
loves stories. One of the most effective means of telling God's story
is to share your story. One way is to outline the times in your life,
both highs and lows, when God has intervened and revealed himself
to you. This is your testimony of God's work in your life. Keep it
simple. Avoid including details understood only in your cultural
context. Give highlights that illustrate the truth of the good news—
that God loves sinners and has sent Jesus to take the punishment
for our sin; that we can have a relationship with God if we confess
our wrong doings and accept that Jesus is the only provision to
reestablish our relationship with God; and what that relationship
means to you in your everyday life. Our lives are not perfect because
we are Christians. The truth is that we need Jesus in our lives every
moment of every day. Practice sharing with others what God is
doing in your life. The blessing you have received will be multiplied
when shared with another, and the glory will belong to God.

Contextualization
A common picture of an evangelical Christian is that of a fanatic,
crazy person standing on the street corner preaching about Jesus.
Missionaries are depicted as insensitive people who have their own
agendas and are clueless regarding another culture. Books like
The Poisonwood Bible and *Hawaii* reinforce these pictures. Christian
missionaries are accused of destroying cultures by bringing their
own culture and values to primitive peoples. These pictures and
accusations contain elements of truth. Missionaries have not always

been culturally sensitive. They have not always listened to and observed the people to whom they are bringing the good news.

A church leader with whom I worked in Uganda said to me, "Before I became a Christian, I was a teacher and had several wives. In order to attend the seminary, the missionaries told me that I could have only one wife. So I put aside all of my wives except for the one I have. Then I went to seminary and studied the Bible. There I learned that Abraham, Jacob, David and Solomon had many wives. I began to wonder what else that the missionaries had taught me was not true." He later left the church in disgrace.

Mack and Leeann Stiles write, "God is not a Westerner. He is the Lord of all the earth. God knows all cultures intimately. God, therefore, is the author of cultural sensitivity. We desire to understand other cultures because God knows other cultures. We want to speak in the framework of another person's culture because God spoke in the framework of another's culture. We go to other cultures with the message of redemption as God did rather than requiring other cultures to come to us. We don't ask other cultures to change before they hear the message; rather, we change so that they can hear the message because that's what God did."[2]

When Jesus came to earth to reveal God to us, he became a human being. He spoke the language of the law to the lawyer Pharisees; he used common illustrations to explain the kingdom of God to the common people; he was compassionate toward the poor and the suffering. The great missionary, the apostle Paul, also adapted the message to suit the listener. "To the Jews I became as a Jew, in order to win Jews. To those under the law I became as one under the law (though I myself am not under the law) so that I might win those under the law. To those outside the law I became

as one outside the law (though I am not free from God's law but am
under Christ's law) so that I might win those outside the law. To the
weak I became weak, so that I might win the weak. I have become
all things to all people, I might by all means save some. I do it all for
the sake of the gospel, that I may share in its blessing" (1 Cor 9:20-23).

By assuming the posture of a learner, by carefully observing
customs and interactions and by asking questions and attentively
listening to the responses, we can begin to understand a culture.
This also helps to establish trust. It helps us to earn the right to
share our culture. It helps us to bring the message of Jesus Christ in
culturally appropriate ways.

Prayer
Partnership with God requires regular communication with him.
Prayer is one way you can tell God what is on your mind, how
things are going in your life and what you need. Jesus took time to
pray and communicate with God, his Father. During times of
listening prayer God communicates with us.

Developing a prayer life takes discipline. The work of mission,
especially mission built around health care and medicine, is
extremely tiring, time consuming and fraught with interruptions.
It is easy to get caught in the busyness of the work, the urgency of
the crisis and the lack of resources, both material and human, and
forget to talk to God about these things.

Having the support of people who promise to pray on your
behalf helps cover those times when you are unable to pray.
Cultivate prayer partners as much as financial partners in ministry.
I know that the prayers of my family and supporters carried me
through some difficult times and provided a hedge of protection
around me.

Spiritual warfare

Just before I left Uganda to return to the U.S., a bishop friend stayed in my guest room for a couple of days while he waited for his wife to arrive. One night over supper, I asked him, "Henry, how did you come to know the Lord? I've never heard your testimony." Henry proceeded to share his story. His grandfather was a wizard. They had offered traditional sacrifices before they went fishing. As a young man, he attended the teachers' training school. It was there during a mission that he heard the gospel for the first time with understanding. He then became violently ill for several days. His classmates prayed for him. The demons were battling for his soul. With prayer they left. As he continued, Henry began explaining about a spiritual dimension in which battles were taking place of which I had been totally unaware. God opened my eyes to recall and see how this battle had been going on my entire six years in Uganda. Henry had led all-night prayer vigils during the political unrest. He considered himself a pastor to the missionaries. Indeed, he was. He had studied theology in England and had bridged into British culture. Now he was helping me to bridge into his. In the process a whole new spiritual realm was opened for me.

Over the years, God has gently allowed me to glimpse into the spiritual dimension. I have come to understand that often events that had occurred or that were happening were beyond my intervention. Just as Job was unaware of the dialogue between Satan and God regarding him, so I was unaware of the spiritual battles taking place around me.

Jesus was aware of this battle for our souls. Just before he went to the cross, he prayed, "I have given them your word, and the world has hated them because they do not belong to the world, just as I do not belong to the world. I am not asking you to take them out of the world, but I ask you to protect them from the evil one.

They do not belong to the world, just as I do not belong to the world. Sanctify them in the truth; your word is truth. As you have sent me into the world, so I have sent them into the world. And for their sakes I sanctify myself, so that they also may be sanctified in truth.

"I ask not only on behalf of these, but also on behalf of those who will believe in me through their word, that they may all be one. As you, Father, are in me and I am in you, may they also be in us, so that the world may believe that you have sent me" (Jn 17:14-21).

Suggested Activities

1. Write a personal testimony outlining your spiritual journey.

_____

_____

_____

_____

_____

_____

2. Pray for the people you will be serving, as well as the members of your team.

1 Paul Borthwick, *Missions: God's Heart for the World,* Downers Grove, IL: InterVarsity Press, 2000.

2 J. Mack and Leeann Stiles, *Short-Term Missions*, Downers Grove, IL: InterVarsity Press, 2000, p. 62.

UNIT 3: PREPARING EMOTIONALLY

Objectives
At the end of this unit, you should be able to:
1. Describe culture shock
2. Identify areas of tension when caring across cultures

J esus prayed that we would be one, just as he was one with the Father and the Holy Spirit. The unity among believers is a testimony to the trinity and proclaims the truth of the gospel. The problem is that we are very diverse. While we generally have similar characteristics — two eyes, two ears, one nose, one mouth, two arms, two legs — we also have differences in these characteristics. Some have blue eyes, some have green, some have brown; some have large noses, some have pointed noses, some have flat noses; some have mouths with large lips, some barely have an upper lip, some have been born with cleft lips. To establish individual identities, we focus on the differences, the things that are unique to us as individuals.

I am a Caucasian woman with brown hair and green eyes. When I look at other Caucasians, I tend to look at hair color and eye color to make the distinction between people. When I went to Africa, everyone had dark hair and brown eyes. They also had dark brown skin. Everyone appeared alike. I soon learned that to distinguish between Ugandans, I needed to look at other physical characteristics. The shape of noses, the size of lips and the variations in skin color became important in identification.

Culture shock

When we encounter many, perhaps overwhelming, numbers of differences, as happens when entering a different culture, we experience culture shock. "Culture shock is the conflict a person experiences when living in a culture with a value orientation different from his or her own. These feelings threaten a person's basic belief system and values—a rather intimidating experience."[3]

Generally four stages have been identified for someone experiencing culture shock. The first is *euphoria* or *honeymoon stage*. During this period, everything is new and exciting. The people, though different, are interesting; the work is atypical and challenging; the food is unusual; and the customs are intriguing. For people who go on short-term mission projects of one to two weeks, they only experience this stage of culture shock.

The second stage is *irritation*. All the differences mount. Sensory overload overtakes the ability to deal with the situation. Sights, sounds, smells, people and bumpy roads become irritating and lose their novelty. We begin to miss some comforts of our home culture. Common reactions to this stage include withdrawal, excessive sleeping, irritability, stereotyping of the host culture, hostility and becoming argumentative. A friend recommended that I bring some things that reminded me of home. A pewter vase that belonged to my grandmother, a porcelain statue that was a going-away gift from my nursing students and photographs of my family eased the homesickness that I felt during this stage.

The third stage is *adjustment*. During this time, life in the new culture becomes familiar. A routine is established. A person begins to adopt some of the new culture. In Uganda, driving follows the rules of the road of England—the steering wheel is on the right, and the driver drives on the left side of the road. This causes great disorientation for those accustomed to the opposite state of affairs. Crossing the street can be hazardous to one's health, when looking for cars to come from the other direction. Getting in and out of the correct side of the vehicle, depending on whether I was driving or riding as a passenger, provided numerous reminders that I had not yet adjusted to life in Uganda. One day everything switched in my brain, and I no longer had to actively think about which way to look when crossing the street or which side of the vehicle I needed to enter. Then I knew that I had adjusted to life in Uganda. Coming back to the U.S. was another story.

The fourth stage is *adaptation*. You become bicultural. The new culture is home, and you enjoy explaining your adopted culture to newcomers. Grocery shopping was different in Uganda. There were little shops, called *dukas*, which carried items such as laundry detergent, tinned margarine and coffee. In the market, men and women sold fresh produce and hand-made items. Meat, if available, was butchered early in the morning; fresh baked bread appeared about midday; and fish came late in the afternoon on Tuesday and Friday. Knowledge of these details was essential to planning an excursion to the market. Sharing this knowledge was always part of a new missionary's orientation.

During my six years in Uganda, I had the opportunity to observe many people pass through culture shock. Almost everyone made it through to the adaptation stage without undue trauma. However, the worst case of culture shock that I have observed did not take place in Uganda. It was in Mississippi when the mission organization I worked with hired someone from Los Angeles, California. When we go to another country, we expect things to be different and anticipate that we will need to make adjustments. When we travel within the U.S., we don't expect to experience so much in the way of regional differences. Mississippi could have been an entirely different country as far as my friend was concerned. During the irritation phase, she complained that there was no traffic. L.A. had six-lane highways with bumper-to-bumper traffic, while in Mississippi we had rural roads that, at best, had rush moments.

Southern food is considered by many to be home-cooked and delicious. It also tends to contain large quantities of fat and is often fried. This led to frustration over the lack of healthy alternatives and the lack of ethnically diverse foods. Finding ways to adjust to the lack of entertainment and cultural outlets, appreciating the culinary delicacies and slower pace of life came as adjustment set in. Later, when family visited from L.A., she was able to authoritatively point out the finer points of life in Mississippi.

Tensions

Being prepared and having insight into some of the potential points of stress in a crosscultural move can assist movement through the phases of culture shock. Evaluating these tensions biblically contributes to our spiritual growth.

Sherwood Lingenfelter and Marvin Mayers[4] have described these points of stress as:

- *Tensions about time*
- *Tensions in judgment*
- *Tensions in handling crisis*
- *Tensions over goals*
- *Tensions about self-worth*
- *Tensions regarding vulnerability*

Tensions about time

This is frequently the first noticeable tension someone experiences when moving crossculturally. A slower pace of life and less concern about punctuality can be stressful to a person who is on a short-term mission project and has limited time to experience the host culture. In reality, this is part of the short-term mission experience.

The tension is between persons who are time-oriented and those who are event-oriented. The time-oriented person values keeping to a time schedule to achieve the goals that have been set. The event-oriented person sees the event as important, not the time. For health care personnel from developed countries who are hard working, schedule-driven and goal oriented, the lack of concern about time is a definite frustration. Their thoughts may include: "We have left busy practices and sacrificed valuable time to help people who ordinarily do not have access to our skills. We have limited time, and we want to get as much done as possible in the time we have."

The bus driver who arrives thirty minutes late has "wasted the valuable resource of time." The bus driver, on the other hand, is accustomed to functioning in an event-oriented society. Bringing North American health personnel to a remote village for a day of providing health care to villagers is an event. He knows that the village people will wait for the doctors and nurses to come and that they see this as an event, much like a market day or a festival. Time is not the focus; the event is the focus.

Time management
The members of Scripture Union at Mvara, the local secondary school in Uganda, asked me to do a workshop on "Time Management" during an annual gathering. They thought that because I was from America, I was the expert in time management. To prepare, I read a couple of Christian management books that addressed the topic. I also studied what the Bible had to say about time. I learned that time is a gift from God, a resource that he has given us, even though God is not bound by time. I learned that God is in control of our time and that we are not in control of it as much as we would like to think. Ecclesiastes 3:1 says, "For everything there is a season, and a time for every matter under heaven." I found that God is egalitarian about time; everyone is given the

same amount. Everyone has 60 minutes in every hour, 24 hours in every day, 7 days in every week and 365 days in every year. When I pointed out these facts to the students, some of them disagreed with me. "You have more time," they said. The perception was that because Americans lived longer, they had more time, and that is why Americans were more successful. I had to agree that our life expectancies were longer, but that was no guarantee that all of us had the expected number of years. Basically, we all had the same amount of time each day God gave us life.

I went on to describe the typical day at the diocesan offices. Each morning began at 8:00 a.m. with devotions, which only four or five men managed to attend. As various people arrived at the office, they would greet those who were there. The greetings are rather lengthy, and getting to everyone took considerable time. It was close to 10:00 a.m. when everyone settled into his or her work. The British custom of having morning tea at this time meant that work stopped while we had tea. Some people who hadn't had breakfast looked for something to eat. That took until 11:00 a.m. The staff worked until noon, when it was time to return home for lunch. Because lunch required building a fire to cook food, the staff often did not begin to return to the office until 2:00 p.m. This necessitated a round of afternoon greetings, also quite lengthy, so a concentrated work effort did not begin until 3:00 p.m. Office hours ended at 4:00 p.m.

By the end of my description, the students were laughing so hard, they could hardly keep their seats. They recognized the truth of what I described. We talked about how Americans frequently did not go through the greeting ritual before jumping into business. One of the students acknowledged that they thought this was rude. They soon realized that the focus in the Ugandan culture was more on the event rather than on time. I explained that in America,

people are paid by the hour for their work. When they learned
that lawyers could charge $200 or more per hour for their services,
they understood the expression "Time is money." For the American
lawyer, a 15-minute greeting was equivalent to $50, a month's
salary in Uganda.

What do you value?

So, who is right? The Ugandans who value the event, or the
Americans who value time? If we look at Jesus as the example, we
see him focusing on the people and events rather than on the time.
He delays his trip to Jairus's house to find out who touched his
cloak and to provide total healing for the woman with the issue of
blood. Jesus did not immediately run to Bethany to heal Lazarus
when he received word that Lazarus was ill. The culture in which
Jesus lived was probably an event-oriented culture. Jesus knew that
time was a gift and that God provides all that we need to do the
work to which he has called us, including the resource of time.

Tensions in judgment

Meetings in Uganda fascinated me. I was accustomed to faculty
and committee meetings where we followed an agenda. Reports
were given, new business introduced and decisions made on each
agenda item. Lingenfelter and Mayers[5] label this type of thinking as
dichotomistic. It has also been called analytic, Greek or Western.
It divides problems into the constituent parts and decisions into
right and wrong options.

   A meeting in the village never followed those rules. The lack
of time-orientation meant that no one came to the designated
meeting place until they heard the engine of our Land Rover
approaching. For the next hour or so, while they prepared themselves for the meeting, we had tea. I learned to carry writing

materials or handwork to make use of this time. The leader would introduce us and the purpose for our visit. My colleagues would explain why we had come. Then the discussion would take place. All aspects of the program would be presented. Discussion would move back and forth between points until a consensus could be ascertained, and the meeting ended. For me it seemed like endless discussion. Sometimes we went on for hours, especially if there were controversial points or items not easily understood or decided. I would begin to wonder if anything would be concluded. Then, suddenly, we would be closing in prayer. I usually had to ask Margaret, my colleague, what they had agreed. She always knew.

This type of meeting represents holistic thinking. Holistic thinkers need to see the whole picture before making a decision. All the positive and negative aspects need to be presented before judgment can be made. This kind of thinking has also been called synthetic, Hebrew or non-Western.

One benefit of ministering crossculturally is the opportunity to appreciate both types of thinking. When I attend an African-American worship service, I can appreciate how the preacher circles around a point and presents it from different angles (a holistic approach). When I'm in my home church, I appreciate a three-point sermon (a logical, linear approach).

Tensions in handling crisis
Those of us who are risk-avoidant constantly plan ahead, trying to prevent problems. Nurses excel at this. We have been educated to anticipate needs and provide for them, prepare for problems before they occur and have pat answers for anything that might occur. When we find something that works, we use it again and again. We are crisis-oriented.

Then there are people who seem to go through life oblivious to potential crises, thinking, "Why worry about something that may never happen?" If a crisis occurs, they prefer to call upon their experience rather than ask an expert to address it. Often, if the first option doesn't work, they'll proceed to a second option. They are non-crisis-oriented. For those who are crisis-oriented, we feel as if we're bailing out our friends who are not crisis-oriented.

In Uganda, I was often on plan B or plan C before I achieved what I needed to accomplish. Several times it went to plan E or plan F. Part of my work in Uganda was assisting my Ugandan colleagues with their planning skills. A location on the equator with fairly fixed amounts of daylight and the trauma of living day to day during the civil war had contributed to a lifestyle of "take it as it comes." Setting goals within realistic time frames, as well as anticipating problems and providing for them, was the challenge to beginning and managing sustainable health programs.

I must admit, however, that I learned to enjoy living more "in the moment" while in Uganda. Not worrying about what the next day would bring was a relief at times, especially when there was nothing I could do about it. Jesus' teaching about worry and God's provision for us is instructive: "And why do you worry about clothing? Consider the lilies of the field, how they grow; they neither toil nor spin, yet I tell you, even Solomon in all his glory was not clothed like one of these. But if God so clothes the grass of the field, which is alive today and tomorrow is thrown into the oven, will he not much more clothe you — you of little faith? Therefore do not worry, saying, 'What will we eat?' or 'What will we drink?' or 'What will we wear?' For it is the Gentiles who strive for all these things; and indeed your heavenly Father knows that you need all these things. But strive first for the kingdom of God and his righteousness, and all these things will be given to you as well. So do not worry about tomorrow, for tomorrow will bring worries of its own. Today's trouble is enough for today" (Mt 6:28-34).

In Proverbs 16:9 we read, "The human mind plans the way, but the LORD directs the steps." God intends for us to plan ahead. Jesus says, "For which of you, intending to build a tower, does not first sit down and estimate the cost, to see whether he has enough to complete it? Otherwise, when he has laid a foundation and is not able to finish, all who see it will begin to ridicule him, saying, 'This fellow began to build and was not able to finish' " (Lk 14:28-30). Jesus made this statement in relation to counting the cost of following him. In ministry we must be certain that it is God who is leading and providing direction. Time in prayer and in the Bible is critical to discerning God's plan. I have attended many meetings that opened with a brief prayer followed by several hours of planning. At the end, we prayed that God would bless our plans. Gratefully, he is a redeeming God and can use even these ill-conceived plans for his benefit. But I'm learning to turn that around by spending long periods of time with God before planning and then being prepared to plan and to act when he directs. That is more in line with what he intends. I'm learning to trust him and allow him to lead my life.

Tensions over goals

I was on an academic career track when God rerouted my life to Uganda. I loved teaching and feel that it is one of the gifts that God has given me. What I loved most about teaching was building into the lives of students. It was fun watching them progress from insecure students to competent professionals. As the faculty advisor to the student Nurses Christian Fellowship chapter, I was able to see growth in their spiritual lives. With students, I attended two Urbana Missionary Conferences, sponsored by InterVarsity Christian Fellowship. I had gone into nursing thinking I would become a missionary and that perhaps God would open the door during those conferences. Instead, I felt him leading me to prepare nurses for mission work. Thus I pursued the academic path.

During graduate school, the diploma school of nursing in which I was teaching became a baccalaureate nursing program. I was intimately involved in the feasibility study, writing the philosophy for the program and curriculum development. During this time I sensed a change in focus — we were increasingly concerned about the profession of nursing. We wanted to be certain that our baccalaureate nursing program provided excellent professional nursing education. I was growing restless and dissatisfied. One day after completing my master's program, while reading my Bible and praying, I realized that when we get to heaven, there would be no need for nursing. Somehow, during the transition from diploma to baccalaureate nursing education, the focus had shifted from the nursing student to the nursing profession. God was saying to me that people — students — had eternal value. He wanted my purpose in life to mesh with his. I was to use my life to build his purposes into the lives of others. He then opened the door to Uganda and allowed me to serve him there by developing community health programs. When I arrived in East Africa, five of my former students were already there!

What I experienced was a tension in goals. Some people are task-oriented. They focus on achieving their objectives and completing their projects. For persons involved in academia, completing degrees, writing curricula and publishing research are driving goals. Often they are workaholics, sacrificing relationships to complete the task. They seek like-minded people who share their achievement-oriented lifestyle. They accomplish great things.

People or tasks?
This is in contrast to people who are person-oriented. They prefer to be with people. The task-oriented person might call them social butterflies — flitting and fluttering around, never getting anything

accomplished. They value the social interaction and would rather be with others who enjoy being in a group.

The tension in a medical mission situation is when a group of highly skilled, achievement-oriented, type-A health professionals arrive in a culture that is person-oriented. Sitting around drinking tea doesn't accomplish anything for task-oriented health professionals. They have come to see patients, do surgery and heal people. They have goals related to the number of people they can help and surgeries they can perform within the time frame they are there. Building relationships with national health professionals and the local hosts is often secondary. Acknowledging that the host culture values the interaction with guest health professionals as much as it appreciates the tasks accomplished goes a long way in contributing to the success of any medical mission project.

How did Jesus handle the tension of goals? Jesus recognized that the people whom he came to save were important. He did not limit the times when he could interact with them. Nicodemus came in the night. Friends lowered their handicapped companion through the ceiling while he was teaching. When he was with his disciples, he shared his life. He built his life into the lives of the disciples, knowing that they would be responsible for carrying on the work when he had returned to heaven. But he also had a task to accomplish. He was taking on the sins of humankind and paying for them on the cross. He balanced the current relationships with people with the task of saving them.

We need to follow Jesus' example. Jesus knew that his time was short. He knew that if his mission were to succeed, it would depend on the disciples he left behind to carry on the work. We need to abandon the *vidi, veni, vinci* — I came, I saw, I conquered — approach and take on the attitude of Christ, that of a humble servant, sharing our human existence and imparting heavenly values and wisdom to his followers and allowing them to carry on the mission.

My role in Uganda was to work myself out of a job. There were many pressures to accomplish tasks. I was constantly asked for numbers: how many people we were serving, how many children under five were malnourished, how many children were saved from dying before their first birthdays and how much *bang for the buck* we were getting. Program success was measured from the task-oriented, achievement-focused funding agencies. The temptation was to get things done, even if I had to do them myself. However, if I were to leave at that point, the program would have ended. God blessed me with capable and competent Ugandan nurse colleagues. I knew that if programs were going to continue after I left Uganda, they would be the ones who carried them on. I needed to impart to them the values, knowledge and skills necessary to plan and implement primary health care programs. To do this, I needed to learn about the culture, understand motivations and appreciate the assets they brought to the table. It meant becoming person-oriented and building relationships to achieve the task of beginning sustainable health programs.

Tensions about self-worth
The American culture is individualistic and achievement-oriented. The U.S. is viewed as the land of opportunity. We believe that even the person at the lowest socioeconomic level can eventually become the president of the United States. We hold up President Lincoln as a model. After all, with enough hard work and determination, everyone should be able to succeed. Social status and self-worth are based on accomplishments. The number of letters behind our name, the books we have published and the money in our bank accounts all reflect individual achievement.

In many cultures, however, social status is ascribed by birth. Who your parents and grandparents were determines your social position. Your identity is tied to your clan, and you are expected to contribute to the clan identity and live up to its standards. This was difficult for me to understand and accept in Ugandan culture.

We had no lawnmowers in Uganda, and my compound had a large yard. Living in the tropics also meant that grass and weeds grew rapidly. To keep them under control, I hired a young man, Peter, who slashed the grass and kept the garden. The civil war had interrupted his schooling. He was a bright young man, who desperately wanted to finish secondary school. I agreed to pay for his school fees if he could find a school that would admit him. But I also expected him to keep the grass slashed and the garden free from weeds. He agreed. One day I found Peter's brother, Steven, slashing the grass. When I asked why he was doing Peter's work, he replied, "If my brother has an opportunity to go to school, then it is my responsibility to help him and do his work." I later learned that the salary I paid Peter for garden work was pooled with the family money and spent according to the priorities they mutually agreed upon. My housekeeper had recommended Peter to me. She told me, "He comes from a good family. He won't steal from you. If you ever want to know who can be trusted, ask me. I know the families that can be trusted."

In our politically correct culture, labeling people by the family to which they were born would not be tolerated. Who we are is determined by what we do as individuals. Is this biblical? How does the Bible ascribe self-worth? First, it says that, in and of ourselves, we are hopeless sinners. "There is no one who is right-eous, not even one; there is no one who has understanding, there is no one who seeks God. All have turned aside, together they have become worthless; there is no one who shows kindness, there is not even one" (Rom 3:10-12). In spite of this reality and out of his unconditional love for us, God still finds us worthy and seeks a relationship with us. By accepting the gift of God's grace through his Son, Jesus Christ, we become adopted into God's family. "Just as he chose us in Christ before the foundation of the world to be holy and blameless before him in love. He destined us for adoption as his children through Jesus Christ, according to the good pleasure of his will, to the praise of his glorious grace that he freely bestowed on us in the Beloved" (Eph 1:4-6). God determines our self-worth. We are his children, and he ascribes our worth. Recognizing that it cost God the Father the death of his Son, Jesus Christ, to adopt me into his family, communicates how valuable I am to him. Neither cultural means of ascribing self-worth—that of achievement or that of ascribing-worth by birth—are scriptural.

As North American Christians, we often think that what we do for God will somehow increase our self-worth. As missionaries we may subconsciously think that we are somehow better than others or that we should have an increase in our social status because of our service to God. The church often contributes to this by setting missionaries on a pedestal. We define *who we are* by *what we do*, instead of allowing *who we are* to define *what we do*. Jesus Christ should be our model. "Let the same mind be in you that was in Christ Jesus, who, though he was in the form of God, did not regard equality with God as something to be exploited, but emptied himself, taking the form of a slave, being born in human likeness. And being found in human form, he humbled himself and became obedient to the point of death—even death on a cross" (Phil 2:5-8). As children gifted by the most high God, we live our lives in his service, doing those things that he has gifted and called us to do out of our love for him and not to increase our self-worth.

Tensions regarding vulnerability
Understanding our identity in Christ helps us to deal with the final area of tension: that of exposing our vulnerability. No one likes to fail. However, cultures handle failure and deal with it differently.

In the U.S., we generally accept failure as part of taking the risks necessary to succeed. We appreciate it if someone who has found a weakness or flaw in our personality or our work approaches us privately and confronts us directly. Exposing vulnerability, while not a pleasant experience, is accepted. We learn from failure, pick up and move on. In other cultures failure is a personal affront and brings shame. People in these cultures prefer suitable mediators rather than direct confrontation. Vulnerability is to be concealed from the person offended or hurt. Of all the cultural *faux pas* that are made in crosscultural ministry, this is the easiest to make unknowingly.

Soon after my arrival in Uganda, I stumbled into a most uncomfortable situation. A colleague had been given a monetary advance for a trip. She was told that she would be required to account for the money with receipts when she returned. After realizing the discrepancy between the amount receipted and the amount of the advance, I confronted her privately. There was an unbearable silence for what seemed like eternity. I finally excused the variance with an acknowledgment that it was difficult to get receipts for purchases made in the market and elsewhere.

I soon discovered it would have been much better to send someone mutually known to us to ask about the problem. She could have made her explanation and/or rectified the problem without exposing her vulnerability. While the confrontation strained our relationship, I was grateful that it didn't end it.

Exposing or concealing one's vulnerability has both positive and negative dimensions. In cultures that expose vulnerability, such as North America, we have the freedom to take risks and benefit from the progress that occurs; however, we also can be careless. For cultures that conceal vulnerability, it is difficult to get to know a person intimately, and problems are often not made known until it is too late to deal with them. On the other hand, cultures that conceal vulnerability will do everything possible to avoid failure and confrontation.

Regardless of the cultural bent toward vulnerability, as Christians we must remember that we are all sinners, saved by grace, and that we need to be sensitive to each other and seek to build one another in Christ rather than focus on our failures and weaknesses. Being culturally sensitive in this area, being willing to use a culturally appropriate means of exposing vulnerability, can be an area of growth for everyone involved in ministering crossculturally. Jesus sent a Mediator in the person of the Holy Spirit to guide us and help us in these situations. "Likewise the Spirit helps us in our weakness; for we do not know how to pray as we ought, but that very Spirit intercedes with sighs too deep for words. And God, who searches the heart, knows what is the mind of the Spirit, because the Spirit intercedes for the saints according to the will of God. We know that all things work together for good for those who love God, who are called according to his purpose" (Rom 8:26-28).

Experiencing tensions in these areas produces growth. We grow personally by having our cultural biases uncovered so they can be examined in the light of Scripture. We grow in our relationships with others by appreciating the differences that exist, possibly adopting the strengths of another culture into our lives. Finally, we grow spiritually in our relationship with God as we learn about the diversity of the people he has created and loved, and as we trust him to help us overcome these tensions.

Dealing with frustration

As part of my orientation to living crossculturally, my mission agency taught a session on frustration. Ministering crossculturally and dealing with the tensions inherent in crosscultural ministry inevitably leads to a certain amount of frustration. They explained that frustration comes from unmet expectations. We were instructed that whenever we felt frustrated, we should consider what we expected in the situation. It was a good lesson. By examining expectations, I could determine whether the expectation was realistic, something that I could change or something I needed to change. Culture is difficult to change, and any expectations I had related to the tensions I experienced from differences in culture had to be accepted. My Ugandan midwife colleague had her own pace and, as much as I tried, she would not be hurried or rushed. I soon realized that she was not going to change, so the only thing that my attempts to change her were going to accomplish was an ulcer or high blood pressure for me. I was the one who needed to change.

Most of my frustration, however, did not come from the cross-cultural aspects of ministry. I expected differences and was willing to adjust my expectations for those differences. Frustration most commonly came from fellow missionaries. Over and over, I became extremely frustrated because I had expectations of them that they did not meet. We shared a culture, American, and a subculture, a denominational church founded by Dutch immigrants. We were supposed to work together, share common objectives and have similar values. Whenever my fellow missionaries did not behave the way I thought they should, I became frustrated, which led to anger, bitterness and disappointment. Examining my expectations and adjusting them to suit those with whom I labored eased tensions.

Suggested Activity:

Complete the personal profile questionnaire, pages 76 to 83 to identify potential tension areas in crosscultural ministry.

---

3 Bonnie Petersen, "Surviving Culture Shock: Lessons Learned as a Medical Missionary in Jamaica," *Journal of Emergency Nursing*, 1995; 21: 505.

4 Sherwood G. Lingenfelter and Marvin K. Mayers, *Ministering Cross-Culturally: An Incarnational Model for Personal Relationships*, Grand Rapids, MI: Baker Book House, 1986.

5 Ibid.

UNIT 4: PREPARING PROFESSIONALLY

Objectives
At the end of this unit, you should be able to:
1. Discuss the various nursing roles in mission settings
2. Present the professional preparation necessary for the various nursing roles

B eing a missionary nurse with North American creden-
tials does not automatically qualify you to practice in
another country. All the restrictions regarding who may
legally practice nursing in North America also apply to nursing in
other countries. That includes obtaining the necessary credentialing
to practice in the host country. Nurses have worked hard to guarantee public safety and assure standards of nursing care in our country.
Nurses in other countries have done the same. As Christian nurses
we seek to serve God and the recipients of our care with excellence.
Just as we do not allow nurses from other countries to practice
nursing in the U.S. without becoming licensed and credentialed, so
we must also seek to become licensed and credentialed in our host
countries. In some countries, this may require additional education
or to serve an apprenticeship or internship to learn about the health
care system of the host country. I've heard some nurses say that the
host government "just wants to get free labor out of missionary
nurses" or other disparaging remarks. Others have welcomed this
as an opportunity to learn more about the country's health system
and culture and to make friends with national nurses. The attitude
with which we approach credentialing communicates our respect
and professional support for the national nurses.

Sometimes it is difficult to get information regarding licensure
in a country. It took several meetings and a lot of questions before I

found the registrar in charge of licensure in Uganda. I was prepared with copies of my transcripts, my Illinois nursing license, a work permit for the country and my curriculum vitae, which I presented to the authorities. When the registrar examined them, she asked questions about nursing education, the licensing process and my nursing experience in the U.S. Then she shared the challenges of nursing in Uganda—the limited resources with which she had to function and the complexities of working within the Ministry of Health. She told me that she knew many missionary nurses who had not bothered to see her and were practicing without licenses. She appreciated the effort I had made to seek licensure and the contribution I was making to nursing in Uganda.

Most responsible short-term medical mission projects will seek permission from the host government for the members of their team to practice professionally while on the project. You should be prepared to provide the documentation requested to gain this permission. It is your responsibility to make sure that you are practicing legally within the host country. While staying in another country, you are subject to the laws of that country. Being a U.S. citizen and licensed to practice nursing in your state does not automatically transfer to the laws and nursing practice in the country you are visiting. Sometimes nurses go on mission trips that do not require them to practice professionally, i.e. a construction project or evangelism team. In these instances, it may not be necessary to obtain a nursing license or permission to practice nursing.

Advanced practice nursing
In many countries, national nurses function in independent roles in clinics and rural health centers. They diagnose and treat common illnesses; they provide prenatal care and deliver babies; they are the most educated health professional for many miles. They are familiar

with the tropical parasitic diseases that health professionals in North America rarely see. They know and understand the family and cultural values.

The practice in these settings differs significantly from a clinic or outpatient setting in North America. Common equipment such as sphygmomanometers, stethoscopes, thermometers, oto-ophthalmoscopes etc. may not be available and should be included in the medical equipment a nurse brings to the field. Nurses who know that they will be functioning in these settings would do well to prepare by learning about the common health problems and their treatment protocols and gaining the necessary skills for professional practice. The lack of diagnostic tests and services requires a greater reliance on physical assessment skills and knowledge of disease presentations. A careful history and physical examination is critical to arriving at an accurate diagnosis and correct treatment. The pressure of long lines at a clinic and the use of language interpreters who may or may not be able to translate medical terminology add to the challenge of providing quality health care. For example, it is not uncommon to have all fevers treated as malaria with chloroquin and aspirin. While malaria is often the most common cause of fever, not all fevers are caused by malaria. By assuming that a fever is caused by malaria and treating for malaria, a nurse may be delaying treatment for another condition.

Many good books can assist the advanced practice nurse in a clinic setting. *Where There Is No Doctor* by David Werner is a classic missionary handbook.[6] Daniel Fountain has written *Primary Diagnosis & Treatment: a Manual for Clinical and Health Center Staff in Developing Countries* [7] published for MAP International by Macmillan Press. The Christian Medical & Dental Association gives its missionaries going on short-term medical mission trips with Global Health Outreach a copy of *Handbook of Medicine in Developing Countries*.[8]

The nursing education of national nurses is often limited, with few opportunities for continuing education. They do the best they can with the educational and material resources that they have. Advance practice nurses who have the privilege of working with national nurses have opportunities to share their knowledge and skills with their national counterparts and to learn about the cultural aspects of health from them.

If you plan to take medical supplies and pharmaceuticals from North America, the following considerations may be helpful:

- The cost of shipping medical supplies often exceeds their value. Check to see if these supplies or alternatives are available for purchase in country or nearby and consider supporting the local economy. If they are not available locally, numerous organizations assist mission agencies in the procurement and shipping of medical supplies. (See list of organizations at the NCF website, www.ncf-jcn.org.)

- In the case of electrical equipment, check hardware and voltage compatibility.

- Many pharmaceutical companies donate drugs that are about to expire. Even though they may still be safe and effective, host countries may refuse to import expired drugs. As Christian health professionals, we don't want to communicate that the people we serve in the host country are less valuable, and therefore can be given expired drugs, than the people we serve in the U.S.

- The World Health Organization has encouraged countries to make a list of pharmaceuticals needed in their country. Some countries will not allow drugs that are not on their lists into the country, with good reasons. Often drugs make their way into the marketplace where people may not know their proper use. Also, medical personnel in other countries

may not be familiar with the pharmaceuticals, especially
combination drugs, used in the U.S. and therefore may
prescribe them inaccurately.

- Some drugs and medical supplies are mostly water. These are
  expensive to transport. Unit dose packaging and sample packaging
  take up space and adds weight. If you have the benefit of
  a pharmacist on your team, consult with him/her about
  repackaging and/or preparing solutions and syrups in country.

In developing countries, disease and illness are often given spiritual
interpretations or may have family and community implications.
One explanation for a person having HIV/AIDS in Uganda was
that someone had neglected to pay a bride price. Malnutrition was
often attributed to a curse put on the child by a first wife. Western
medicine is often viewed as an adjunct to traditional medicine or a
"last resort" when all else fails. An understanding of the culture
and beliefs is necessary to addressing the health education needs
that will lead to changes in health practices or compliance with
prescribed therapy. In cultures that have not made the distinction
between the spiritual world and the physical world, the nurse
needs to realize that the medical care provided may have spiritual
interpretations to the patient. As Christians we need to make it clear
that it is God who is the healer, not the provider or the medicine.

Hospital nursing

Mission hospitals are an integral part of the history of medical
mission. As missionaries brought the message of the gospel of Jesus
Christ around the world, they began churches and built schools so
people could learn to read the Scriptures and hospital personnel
could care for the sick. Missionary nurses often were responsible for
the staffing and administration of these hospitals.

Hospital nursing in mission settings has similarities to hospital nursing in the U.S. There are different units—medical, surgical, pediatrics, and so on—that need to be staffed. Nursing procedures require the skills that we have learned and practiced. There are many differences as well. Families may provide the physical care and feeding of patients and stay with the patient on the ward. This is positive in that the family is available for consultation, teaching and relieving the nursing workload. It can be challenging, in that families will need a place to sleep and, often, to cook. The cost of supplies or the lack of supplies may necessitate reusing equipment instead of using disposable equipment. More attention must be paid to cleaning and sterilization. If care and sterilization of equipment has not been part of your previous nursing experience, reviewing these procedures in preparation is a good idea.

Creativity and problem solving help to meet the challenge of limited resources. I have seen local brewing equipment used to make distilled water for intravenous solutions and tin cans reshaped into fetoscopes. Many North American nurses are shocked at the conditions under which nurses practice and may be critical of the quality of nursing care compared to North American standards. You will need to discern between standards that are critical to a patient's welfare and those that can be relaxed in light of the limita-tions faced in the host country. Missionary nursing requires flexibility and adaptability.

Missionary nurses are often heavily involved in the adminis-tration and personnel issues of the hospital. Management in crosscultural settings can be difficult. Most mission hospitals require some financial subsidy from donors. Mission hospitals usually have limited financial resources and may pay staff wages that will not support their families. The disparity between the resources that missionaries bring with them and their national counterparts can create problems. Missionaries may appear to demonstrate paternalistic attitudes and even arrogance toward national staff. Many administrative issues can be difficult to address in any setting, and are magnified in a crosscultural situation. Before voicing constructive criticism, visiting short-term mission personnel ought to realize that they may not understand the entire dynamic involved in keeping a mission hospital functioning.

Many short-term medical mission trips include surgeons who go to a country to perform surgery. Often local physicians have screened the patients for the types of surgery that they know the visiting surgeons can provide. Specialists in areas such as orthopedics, ENT and plastic surgery are especially welcomed for their knowledge and skills. The visiting surgeons will probably want to serve as many people as they can, as well as teach the local physicians. This requires a surgical team that works well together. The nurses on the team have an important role in making the surgical short-term mission project a success. Nurses who anticipate working in surgery need to be prepared with the knowledge of the types of surgery that will be done, the instruments used and the nursing care pre- and postoperatively.[9] Nurse anesthetists are welcomed as members of these teams and make a valuable contribution.

Public health/community health development

Many of the health problems in developing countries are preventable or can be addressed within the community through education. Expensive hospitals and clinics with their medical interventions may not be required to make a positive impact on the health of a community. A community development approach, raising the overall standard of living within a community, will contribute to the health of the people. There are many entrees into the community to effect community development, including education, economics and housing, as well as health. Better housing, increased income and higher education all correlate with better health. The use of health as a vehicle to promote community development that is initiated and owned by the members of the community is known as community health development. This is accomplished by working with communities, through village health committees, to identify health problems and to train community health workers that the village health committee oversees and supports.

Health professionals in the country where you are serving may be the hardest people to convince about the value of this approach. They have worked hard to learn about caring for and treating people who are ill. Sharing their knowledge with members of the community may mean a loss of prestige and income. On a visit to one of the church clinics in Uganda, I was discussing with the medical assistant (similar to a physician assistant in the U.S.) the large amount of medicine that he was prescribing for parasitic worm infestations. I asked where the people got their drinking water. He told me that their source of water was an unprotected spring. When I suggested that he work with the community to protect the spring, he said, "How will I earn my money if they no longer need medicine?" He had a vested interest in keeping people coming to the clinic.

Even when health professionals are committed to community health development, it may be difficult to release the necessary personnel and resources to work with communities. For example, training traditional birth attendants to identify at-risk pregnancies and to refer them to the hospital or clinic could decrease infant and maternal mortality rates. During my time in Uganda, we trained many nurse midwives to facilitate traditional birth attendant training sessions in the villages. However, their duties within the hospital often took priority over going to the village to teach the traditional birth attendants. A scheduled visit to a community was often postponed when a woman in labor arrived at the clinic. The immediate need to care for the woman in labor took precedence over preventing future complicated pregnancies. Over time, the communities and the traditional birth attendants, who had organized and prepared for their training sessions, lost interest in the training. To facilitate community work, a full-time community nursing position that does not include hospital duties is the ideal.

Community health development work requires a financial commitment. Going to the community entails costly transportation. The pressing financial demands of caring for the sick and injured often usurp funds that have been dedicated to health development work. Taking pictures of gory wounds and complicated medical conditions generates more funding than pictures of healthy children playing football.

Getting a community to focus on health promotion and disease prevention takes much time and energy. If such programs are done well, the community health nurse will probably not be recognized for the effort. Rather, the community will be proud of their accomplishments and claim them for themselves. The goal is to have them own the process and be able to apply it to other situations that require intervention on a community level. As nurses we often get our reward when our patients appreciate the care we provide. In community health development, the reward needs to be the pride the community has in its own accomplishments. The church is in an ideal position to promote health and prevent disease. An example of a church in Honduras that began a health program to address the health needs of a community is presented by Nancy J. Crigger and Lygia Holcomb.[10]

On an evaluation tour of a community where we had trained community health workers, we asked the head of one household,

"What difference have you noticed since the health worker has visited your home?" The health worker had brought us to the home because she had helped the family to improve their health practices by building a latrine, having their children immunized, using a clean water source, etc. The man answered, "We used to visit the clinic at least once a month with a sick family member. Now we haven't been to the clinic in over six months. We have not had to buy medicine for our family." They had improved their health and their income by learning the steps necessary to prevent disease and by taking responsibility for their own health. Getting to this point required repeated visits to the village, discussions with the elders and leaders of the village, training sessions for the community health workers and visits to encourage the health workers. A community health nurse will need skills in non-formal education methods in order to facilitate the ownership and implementation of good health practices. Over time, this will result in a healthier community where health personnel can better serve the people by diagnosing and treating the diseases and conditions that require their knowledge and skills.

Through my work in community health development, I gained a greater appreciation for scriptural truths. Jesus taught the disciples, using non-formal education methods, to bring *shalom* — biblical health and wholeness — to communities that would become the church. Trying to get members of communities to work together gave me a greater appreciation for what it must have been like for Jesus to work with the disciples. Peter, the impetuous one, was ready to jump on the bandwagon without thinking. The dubious Thomas needed proof. James and John squabbled over who would get to sit next to Jesus. Judas betrayed him. Yet each one had an important role in building the church. It is a testimony to God's grace and power that he could use these men to begin the Christian church. Whenever I got discouraged about the people with whom

God gave me to work, I took comfort in the knowledge that Jesus had done it and that it was his work. It is a testimony to God's grace and power that he could use me to bring *shalom* to communities.

Education

So much of nursing involves education — of patients, their families and communities. We also teach nursing assistants and auxiliary personnel (and sometimes physicians). Nurse educators focus on nursing students. Missionary nursing also involves education. What we teach about nursing knowledge and skills, as well as our love for our Lord Jesus Christ, is a legacy we leave behind.

We are moving toward becoming a global village. Nursing is a part of that movement. As nurses from various countries meet, they naturally compare notes and share experiences. In the U.S., awareness is growing that we can learn a great deal from nurses in other countries. They are also eager to learn from us, so nursing education around the world lends itself to missionary endeavors.

The Ministry of Health in Uganda was revising its curriculum for nursing education during my time there. Because of my experience in nursing education in the U.S., I was invited to join the group working on this project. As we talked about a philosophy of nursing, we considered what we believed about the person. I told them of the debates we had among our faculty in the U.S. about the statement in our philosophy "that each person is created in the image of God." We discussed the implications of that statement. For nurses whose culture did not divide people into physical, spiritual, emotional and social beings, this was not an issue. I considered it an honor as a Christian nurse to work with them to update their curriculum to reflect the nursing values and practice required to meet the health needs of their country.

Several years later, the Ministry of Health entered into an agreement with the Rockefeller Foundation and Case Western

Reserve University to begin the first baccalaureate nursing program at Makerere University in East Africa. Two faculty members from Case Western Reserve were sent to Uganda to begin working on the curriculum, while six Ugandan nurses went to the university to obtain master's degrees. Overseas faculty appointments such as these are great opportunities for nurses to become "tent maker" missionaries—Christians employed in secular positions overseas. The nursing program at Makerere is now well established. I recently met a Baptist missionary who is teaching in the Makerere nursing program. She has a wonderful opportunity to integrate her faith with her nursing practice and teach fellow faculty members and nursing students about nursing and Jesus.

The shortage of nursing personnel is often more acute in mission hospitals. Many of them have begun their own nursing education programs that prepare national nurses. Nurse educators have an opportunity to initiate these nursing programs and to teach in them. A Korean-American nurse successfully began a government-approved nursing program at the mission hospital near where I worked. Other mission hospitals have programs that teach nursing assistants.

Missionary nurses need continuing nursing education to maintain their licenses in the U.S. and to remain current in their nursing practice. They appreciate it when continuing nursing education (CNE) offerings are brought to them, and they have an opportunity to meet and study together. Baylor University brought a CNE program to Kenya several years ago that encouraged and educated the nurses in East Africa.

Non-formal education
Formal academic education, in the traditional sense, prepares nurses and auxiliary personnel to function in clinical settings. When working with communities to educate health committees and

community health workers/promoters about health, non-formal or adult education methodologies are more effective. Persons skilled in this method of education focus on facilitating learning and are instrumental in the success of community health development programs. Teaching others how to teach using non-formal education requires practicing the art and skill of facilitation. A facilitator learns from the students as well as facilitating their learning. An understanding of non-formal education methodologies will prove extremely helpful in a crosscultural setting.

Studying how Jesus, the master teacher, taught is a good way to learn more about non-formal education. He often introduced the lesson with a story, a parable. Then he would ask questions about the story to help learners understand and own the point of the lesson. He would then encourage the learners to put into practice the lesson they had learned.

Consider the parable of the Good Samaritan in Luke 10:30-37. The expert in the law tested Jesus by asking, "Who is my neighbor?" Jesus answered by telling the story of a man beaten and robbed on the way to Jericho. A Levite (priest) and a Pharisee (teacher of the law) both pass by without helping. Then an outcast Samaritan comes along; dressed the man's wounds; put him on his donkey; took him to an inn and paid for his care. The story brings home the point that whoever needs assistance is our neighbor and that we are to be a neighbor to everyone who needs our help.

Then Jesus asked the teacher, "Which of these three, do you think, was a neighbor to the man who fell into the hands of the robbers?" The lawyer replied that it is the one who had mercy on the victim. Jesus had the man answer his own question, discovering the answer for himself. Then Jesus said, "Go and do likewise." The objective of non-formal education is to facilitate the learner to own the knowledge, value the lesson and put it into practice.

Suggested Activities:

1. Gather the documents you will need to present to become credentialed in a host country:
   - curriculum vitae
   - nursing license
   - transcripts from educational institutions

2. Study about the common health problems of the country to which you will be going. Begin by checking the website of the Centers for Disease Control and Prevention (CDC) at *http://www.cdc.gov/travel/*.

---

[6] David Werner, *Where There Is No Doctor,* (The Hesperian Foundation, PO Box 1692, Palo Alto, CA, 94302, 1977).

[7] Daniel E. Fountain, *Primary Diagnosis & Treatment*, (MAP International, PO Box 50, Brunswick, GA, 1992).

[8] Catherine Wolf and Dennis Palmer, *Handbook of Medicine in Developing Countries,* (The Christian Medical & Dental Association, PO Box 7500, Bristol, TN, 1999).

[9] Terri Goodman, "Transcultural Nursing: A Personal and Professional Challenge," *Nursing Clinics of North America* 29, no 4: 809-15.

[10] Nancy J Crigger and Lygia Holcomb, "Beyond Band-Aids: Empowering a Honduran Community to Care," *Journal of Christian Nursing 17*, no.1 (Winter 2000): 30-35.

Unit 5: Preparing Physically

Objectives
At the end of this unit, you should be able to:
1. Detail the steps necessary to prepare physically for a health care mission trip
2. Identify potential health risks that occur during an overseas mission trip

You are a whole person. Although spiritual and emotional preparation for a mission trip is extremely important, you must also prepare yourself physically to function effectively.

Pre-trip preparations

Before you can serve in another country, you have to meet their requirements for legal entry and ensure that you will be able to re-enter your country of origin. First, find out if you will need a passport to enter the country where you will be serving. The U.S. Department of State has a helpful website at *http://travel.state.gov/passport_services.html*. Click on "Foreign Entry Requirements" for a listing of the requirements of each country. The site also provides details about applying for a passport, application forms to download and a list of locations that can process the application, including county courthouses and local post offices. You will need to fill out the form, provide the necessary documentation of your birth and citizenship and submit passport photos. Canada maintains a similar website at *http://www.ppt.gc.ca/*. If you are not a citizen of the country from which you are beginning your journey, be sure that leaving the country will not jeopardize your status as a legal resident. It can take several months to get a passport, so begin early.

Some countries require a visa for entry. Visas are obtained from the embassy of the host country. You will need a passport in order to apply for visas from the countries to which you are traveling. Visa services will take your passport to the host country embassies for a fee (*see http://travel.state.gov/visa_services.html*). Most visas require additional fees. This process takes time. Begin at least six months in advance.

Before traveling overseas, see your physician for a physical exam and immunizations against diseases endemic to the areas where you will be traveling. The Centers for Disease Control maintains a website listing health recommendations at *http://www.cdc.gov/travel*. Since some of the immunizations require a series of injections, it is wise to do this at least three months prior to your planned departure. Some countries require proof of immunizations prior to issuing visas. Unless you are traveling with a dental team, a visit to the dentist is a good idea. You don't want to be laid up with a sore tooth.

In tropical areas, malaria is a common health problem. Taking prophylactic medication and precautions against mosquito bites is the best way to prevent malaria. The most common malaria prophylaxis is chloroquin tablets once a week. They need to be started two weeks prior to leaving the country and continued for a time after you return. In places where there is chloroquin-resistant malaria, other drugs may be prescribed. Check the CDC recommendations for the area and consult with local missionaries and physicians about malaria prophylaxis. The type of medication will vary depending on the type of malaria in the area and the length of time you intend to be in the region. Some antimalarial medications have serious side effects and contraindications. I know of several psychotic episodes attributed to antimalarial medications that resolved themselves after the medication was stopped. A treated mosquito net over your bed provides the comfort of knowing you

are protected from mosquitoes while sleeping. Using mosquito
repellents that have less than 30% DEET, especially at dawn
and dusk, also helps.

The first rule of infection control is to wash your hands
frequently, especially before eating and after using the toilet or
handling money. Take an ample supply of any medications that
you need routinely. Take a spare pair of eyeglasses or contact lens-
es. A first-aid kit that contains band-aids, antiseptic solution for
cleaning wounds, cold tablets and painkillers will help prepare for
unforeseen injury or illness. A medication for travelers' diarrhea is
helpful. A portable water filtration unit could be included to provide
a reliable source of clean drinking water. Unless you know that ice
has been prepared from clean water, do not drink beverages that
contain ice. Americans are known throughout the world as people
who like iced drinks, but it is wise to forgo this pleasure when
traveling abroad. Avoid uncooked vegetables or fruits that
cannot be peeled.

Take enough personal hygiene products that you may need,
including shampoo, soap, toothpaste and brush, and feminine
hygiene products. In remote locations these may not be available.
The sun can be especially severe in the tropics. Avoid sun exposure,
use sunscreen and wear a hat and protective clothing. Remember
to drink plenty of fluids. Fluids are lost via insensible perspiration,
and by sweating.

Pack clothing suitable for the climate and culture. Some cultures
do not look kindly on women who wear pants or shorts. After using
pit latrines on a regular basis, I came to appreciate why women
wore skirts. Non-constricting cotton clothing is a good choice for
hot climates. Elevation does make a climatic difference. Uganda is
on the equator, but my home was at nearly 4,000 feet. While it was
occasionally hot, I was more uncomfortable during the summers
I lived in Mississippi. Trips to Nairobi, Kenya, at 7,000 feet, could

be downright cold at night, requiring sweaters and jackets. Comfortable walking shoes are a must. Avoid taking too many items. Airlines limit the number, weight and size of suitcases and carry-on luggage. My rule of thumb is that if I can't carry, wheel or roll whatever luggage with which I am traveling for the distance required to board the airplane, I leave something behind. Checked luggage on international flights with several stopovers frequently gets delayed. Be sure to take medications, personal hygiene items and a change of clothing in a carry-on bag. Remember that knives, scissors, metal nail files and clippers in carry-on baggage will be confiscated. Pack them in your checked baggage, and carry an emery board.

Consider taking a small battery-operated short-wave radio. Listening to the news on the BBC (British Broadcasting Company) or VOA (Voice of America) helps one to keep in touch. You may face travel delays, emergencies and complications that interfere with meals. Include snack bars or trail mix.

Take a camera to record people, places and events on your trip. However, be sensitive to the culture and ask permission before taking pictures. Some countries prohibit photographs of places sensitive to national security such as airports, tall buildings, bridges and dams, so be cautious with your camera in these areas.

Of course a Bible, journal and reading material are essential. A flashlight, called a *torch* in countries with British influence, helps when there is no electricity.

While in host country

When you arrive in your host country, you may find yourself surrounded by unfamiliar sights, smells and sounds. You will probably feel both excited and apprehensive. You may feel over-whelmed with a sense that you are completely out of control if you cannot read signs, ask directions or find a familiar face. Getting through customs and immigration, collecting luggage, meeting new people and getting to the destination is both exhilarating and exhausting. If you have changed time zones, allowing your body to adjust to a new schedule may take several days. The rule of thumb for jet lag is one day of adjustment for each time zone that you have changed. Some people adjust better than others, but it is a good idea to plan time for naps and to expect some sleepless nights if you have traveled across many time zones.

At some time during your travel, you will be using road transportation. A leading cause of death among missionaries is road accidents. Overloaded, poorly maintained vehicles contribute to this, along with reckless driving and not wearing seat belts. Poorly maintained roads and off-road travel also contribute to accidents and injury. Poorly regulated public transportation makes this form of travel risky. Avoid taking any unnecessary risks; however, at times you may need to compromise on some standards if you want to reach your destination.

Prepare for language differences. In Uganda, although English was the official language, it was spoken as a second language by most Ugandans. I was told that forty-five languages were spoken in Uganda. The Madi/West Nile Diocese, with whom I worked, had five language groups. Meetings were translated into all the local languages so people could understand clearly what was being said.

Even their English sounded unfamiliar. Uganda was a British protectorate, so the spoken and written language was British English, which at times seemed like a foreign language to me. We *collected* people when we picked them up; we put *cells* into our *torches* when we put batteries in our flashlights, and trucks were called *lorries*.

Medical language has a specialized vocabulary, and not all interpreters will have the ability to translate medical terms, especially if the interpreter is a child or a family member. Providing health care using an interpreter provides additional challenges. I was surprised to learn how often I used idioms and slang that made no sense when translated literally. Eventually, I learned to eliminate them. Coming from the Midwest, I spoke fast and ran words together, making it difficult for my Ugandan friends to understand. Speaking slowly, without contractions and enunciating clearly became what my American friends call my "Uganda English", but Ugandans could understand me.

It takes a great deal of time to say everything twice, to ensure the accurate translation of what was said, and to have a response translated. If you will be working through an interpreter, you will benefit from Ruth Pakieser's and Mary McNamee's helpful suggestions in their article "How to Work with an Interpreter,"[11] including:

- Know the audience
- Learn a few words of the second language
- Use proper English, avoiding slang
- Use simple, not simplistic, language
- Remember syntax differs among languages
- Speak in full sentences, pausing frequently
- Choose a term and stick with it
- Know the language skills of the interpreter

When speaking through an interpreter, your natural inclination will be to look at the interpreter; however, you are addressing the audience, so be sure to keep your eyes on them.

If you will have access to audiovisual equipment for your presentations, work in advance with a translator to prepare overheads or slides in the language of the people you will be addressing. However, keep in mind that in some countries, electricity may be unreliable and supplies and equipment limited, so do not rely too heavily on audiovisuals.

Avoid jokes and cartoons. Humor is culturally conditioned. Something that seems hilarious to you might come across as serious, or even offensive, in another culture.

If you want to learn patience, humor and humility, try learning another language. Language provides insight into the culture. For example, while attempting to learn Lugbara, I learned that the word for *problem* could be translated literally as "to be called an elephant." This correlated with a legend that talked about different personalities. Problem people were like elephants that stood in the road.

Reentry
A missionary friend gave me good advice about my return to the U.S. She said, "Go with an attitude of serving the people whom you will meet, and do not expect those at home to be interested in your experience." Sure enough, upon returning, I found that those whom I had left behind had carried on with their lives and were more anxious to tell me about what had happened to them while I was away than in hearing about my experience.

It is important to debrief after your missions experience. Plan to get together to share pictures, a meal and reentry experiences with others who went on the trip. The missionary experience, including seeing the poverty of developing countries, learning to live more simply and finding fulfillment in the midst of it, will change your values. Finding someone who is a good listener will help you work through the mission experience. You gain an appreciation for the small things in life, like running water and regular electricity. The relatively affluent lifestyles and abundant consumer goods in America may seem overindulgent. When a missionary friend and I stopped in a shopping mall during her home visit, she looked around at all the glitter and glitz, then said "I can say this to you. Isn't this all a bit much?" If you have been abroad for an extended period of time, it may take some time for you to once again feel comfortable in your own country. A book by Peter Jordan from Youth with a Mission helps with reentry, *Reentry: Making the Transition from Missions to Life at Home.*[12]

Suggested Activities

1. Make a list of items that you will need for the trip.

    a. Ask your sending agency for their recommendations.
        They may have sample packing lists.

    b. Talk to others who have recently traveled to your host country.

    c. Dr. Christine Aroney-Sine, who served as the medical
        director for the Mercy Ships, has written a very readable,
        short book, *Survival of the Fittest*,[13] which gives many
        suggestions on preparing for a mission trip.
        It also includes helpful checklists.

2. Keep a daily journal of your mission experience.

---

[11] Ruth A. Pakieser and Mary McNamee, "How to Work with an Interpreter,"
The Journal of Continuing Education in Nursing 30, no.2 (March/April 1999): 71-74.

[12] Peter Jordon, *Reentry: Making the Transition from Missions to Life at Home*
(YWAM Publishing, P.O. Box 55787, Seattle, WA, 1992).

[13] Christine Aroney-Sine, *Survival of the Fittest* (MARC, 121 East Huntington Drive,
Monrovia, CA, 1994).

Unit 6: Finding a Sending Organization

Objectives
At the end of this unit, you should be able to:
1. Describe the differences between long- and short-term mission assignments
2. Discuss the advantages and disadvantages of a faith missionary position and salaried missionary position
3. Identify key matters to discuss with mission sending agencies

B efore you can embark on a mission, you will need to affiliate with a sending organization. Finding a sending organization that fits you, your skills and your philosophy can seem like a daunting task.

Short-term vs. long-term

An arbitrary definition for short-term might be less than one year. When a nurse agrees to go for less than one year, usually there isn't time to learn a language or invest in sufficient study of the host culture. Most short-term mission trips are one or two weeks up to six months or a year. Some agencies specialize in providing short-term mission trips. They often work with missionaries or agencies within the host country to provide a specific health ministry. A short-term mission experience is a great way to see if you can adapt well in a crosscultural situation or to see if God might be leading you to a longer service term. Many of the mission-sending agencies offer short-term mission programs as a recruiting tool. Many long-term missionaries got to the mission field by first experiencing a short-term mission project. My first encounter with missionary nursing was as a nursing student on a two-week, short-term medical mission to Honduras with the Christian Medical & Dental Association. The year before I went to Uganda as a missionary I visited a nursing school friend who was a missionary in the western part of Uganda. Both trips provided valuable experiences to prepare me for my longer-term commitment.

Long-term mission service might be considered anything longer than a year. Usually if a nurse is going for that length of time, it is necessary to set up housekeeping within the country. A long-term necessitates a significant financial investment in shipping household goods and learning a language to adequately function in the host country, as well as a commitment to understanding the culture. Long-term service requires formalizing your legal status within the country. This means obtaining a work visa rather than a visitor's visa, which often requires working with an organization recognized within the country.

The benefits of short-term mission has been greatly debated in mission circles. It takes a lot of energy and time on the part of the church or missionaries in the country to host a short-term mission group. "Short-termers" are high maintenance. They need to be transported, assisted with documents, provided accommodations, food and water for drinking and bathing. Often this is their first trip outside of their country and they have lots of questions and criticisms. They may have had little or no orientation to the country, which necessitates some orientation to the host culture on the part of their hosts. If the cost of their travel is added to the cost of providing for their time in the country, many missionaries will question the value of the short-termer's contribution to the mission endeavor.

For example, we had a group of teenagers come to Uganda from Ireland one summer to help at the hospital in Kampala. They did some simple repairs and painting, had a few activities with the children and brought great enthusiasm for the Lord. My Ugandan friends asked about how much it cost for the group to come. They suggested that the money could have been put to better use by paying local people to do the work that the teenagers did. This would have helped local people provide for their families. They determined that more work could have been done around the hospital had the money been sent rather than the teenagers. I don't know how the experience affected the Irish teenagers and how God used the experience of visiting Uganda in their lives. Perhaps in God's economy, the money was well spent.

To have a positive short-term mission nursing experience, nurses should seek to participate in mission programs that will utilize their knowledge and skills. Some nurses go on short-term mission projects as part of a team that may or may not be involved in a health-related mission. If the group is a construction team, and you are serving as the nurse, then your responsibilities will be different from going as part of a medical team to provide health services to the local population. It is important to ask medical teams how nurses fit into the team. If it is a surgical team, they may expect you to serve as a scrub nurse. Some projects use nurses in triage or in the pharmacy. Some projects use them in crowd control. If the purpose of the short-term mission is to try on missionary nursing in anticipation of a longer-term commitment, you should try to find a nursing experience that will give you a feel for what you will be doing. Be prepared to be flexible. Even the best-laid plans frequently need to be revised. Go as a learner and a servant. Look for God at work in your life, the lives of your fellow short-term missionaries, and the lives of the people whom you are serving. In general, the short-term missionary usually receives more benefit from the mission experience than those in the host country.

Faith mission vs. salaried position
Many missionary sending agencies require their missionaries to raise their support. This means that you are responsible for soliciting the funds necessary for you to live and work in the country to which you are going. Generally this is done by asking family,

friends, colleagues and churches to make a regular financial commitment to your work. The advantage of this approach is that you not only garner funding but also prayer support. In addition to the accountability you have to the mission agency, you also have accountability to your supporters. Keeping them informed of what God is doing in and through your work with regular communication is an important part of your job and requires a major commitment of time and energy.

Some mission agencies provide a salary for a nursing position. They often receive their funding through denominational contributions or grants from foundations or government agencies such as the United States Agency for International Development (USAID). These agencies contract with nurses for a given period of time that includes some home service time and/or vacation time. During home service, you may be asked to speak to donors. The commitment of the donors is generally to the work of the mission agency. Their interest in you may be limited to your contribution to the mission work. They may or may not take a personal interest in you as their missionary. Foundational or government funding is generally limited to a project, so your employment may be contingent on the availability of funding for the project. This arrangement allows you to focus on the work you have been called to, with the assurance that you will be paid. It also means that you have a fairly reliable source of funding for your work, a working budget rather than a ministry fund built on donations that you solicit for your work.

I have served both as a faith-based missionary and as a salaried missionary. I have found my faith strengthened by God's provision as a faith missionary. I have enjoyed being free to work hard at my job and serve the Lord knowing that the financial needs for the work and me were provided for as a salaried missionary.

Questions to ask

In addition to funding sources, other important questions to
ask mission agencies pertain to doctrinal statements, values and
policies. Usually mission agencies have written statements that
they are happy to provide.

Theological foundations

Doctrinal statements provide a common theological base for a mission
agency. Having missionaries who quarrel over theology on the field
does not draw non-believers to seek a personal relationship with God.
Some doctrinal statements are very specific about controversial
issues such as baptism and eschatology, while others are more basic
creedal statements such as the Apostles' Creed. Taking a close look at
the mission doctrinal statement and examining it in relation to what
you believe should prevent major conflicts. The reason some issues
are controversial is because people interpret the Bible differently. It
may not matter to you one way or the other. However, it may matter
to some of your supporters if you are going with a faith mission.
When I went to Uganda, I sought a position with an agency whose
doctrinal position was consistent with my church's doctrinal statement.
I felt that I could not ethically ask my church to support me in an
agency whose doctrine differed from theirs.

Sending agency values

Mission values are a little harder to ferret out. I found over time
that certain values were extremely important to me and that I was
more comfortable working with people who shared those values.
For example, I strongly value integrity and refuse to compromise
integrity for expediency. In one situation I was asked to extrapolate
numbers to represent larger populations and thus greater numbers
of people served by a project. I refused.

Quality of care and quantity of care can be conflicting values. Some people value seeing lots of patients in a day as a measure of success, while others value taking quality time with people and tending to their spiritual needs, as well as to their physical, social and emotional needs. Lifestyle has its values. As a missionary, will you try to recreate North America with all of its accoutrements, or do you seek to fit into the culture and live a more modest lifestyle? Is the mission agency committed to long-term development and community ownership of health, or do they require immediate results for their funding sources? Defining and refining your values and aligning them with your mission colleagues will give you a more satisfying mission experience.

Most mission organizations have policies on topics such as hostage taking, bribing and evacuation from the country in the event of political instability or natural disaster. Most agencies state that they will not negotiate with hostage-takers for the release of missionaries. Some mission agencies prohibit any bribing. In developing countries where bribing is expected, these policies can cause problems on many fronts, such as travel, customs, licenses and work permits. Some mission agencies have policies on the exchange of currency through the black market. When there is great disparity between the official exchange rates and the black market rates, market prices are usually based on the "unofficial" exchange rate and can reduce purchasing power within a country.

Disciplinary policies
It is important to know on what basis a missionary would be asked to leave. While we like to think that missionaries are all solid citizens and strong in their faith, they face the same temptations and sometimes succumb to them. Asking about disciplinary policies and procedures is reasonable. For example, how has the mission agency

dealt with such issues as use of alcohol or tobacco, sexual activity outside of marriage or suspected abuse? What appeal procedures are available if you feel falsely accused?

Family support

What support does a mission agency offer to families? If you are married, you will want to know the expected roles for spouses and children. Being single doesn't mean that you don't have a family. How does the mission agency help you to maintain your family relationships as a single person? What policies do they have for emergency leaves, especially if you should need to provide long-term care for a family member? The stresses of living with limited resources in another culture, especially in politically unstable countries, can be emotionally taxing. During one term in Uganda, the country was fighting a civil war, I lost both a Ugandan colleague and a mission colleague in road accidents and faced the onslaught of work in the HIV/AIDS crisis. I appreciated that my mission agency offered a visit with a psychologist upon my return to the States. It was helpful to debrief with an objective, independent (not related to the mission agency) person. I needed spiritual support as well, and deeply appreciated pastoral visits from the mission home office, as well as from Ugandan pastor friends. Mission agencies often have personnel dedicated to *member care.* Inquiring about these services will help you determine whether this mission agency will fit with your expectations.

Finances

Finally, there is the issue and reality of finances. You have a right to ask the mission agency for an audited financial report. You need to know that the agency is on sound financial footing before you go abroad and that its accounting practices are in line with common practices and laws pertaining to them. If you are going as a faith missionary, your donors will want to know that information. It is common practice to take a percentage of donations designated for your support as overhead expenses. This is to cover the costs of receiving and receipting donations, postage, member care support and other essential services. Ask the mission agency what percentage of donations goes toward overhead and what that overhead covers. Questions related to health, disability and life insurance should be addressed. God does provide for all our needs, but he usually works through appropriate systems. I believe that he expects us be responsible for addressing these concerns.

Church-to-church partnerships
Over the past few years, a new trend has evolved. Churches are sending missionaries to the field directly and do not use a sending mission agency. Some churches are developing church-to-church partnerships and sending people between countries. There are many reasons for this new trend. Among them is the benefit of direct involvement with what God is doing in another culture. As with all new developments, this one has its pluses and minuses. The accountability is directly to the church and its authority. However, most churches are not expert in mission. Too many church-sent missionaries are not adequately prepared in cultural competency. Another risk is that the church may not offer all the services that mission sending agencies provide for their missionaries, including support, member care and legal advice related to living abroad. Christian churches around the world are sending missionaries. I have met missionaries in the U.S. from Nigeria. Korea sends missionaries around the world. They are facing some of the same challenges that the churches in Europe and the U.S. have faced over the years and are gaining an appreciation for the complexity of God's kingdom-building work.

Mission philosophy

Over the years, I have developed a philosophy of mission that helps me define what I believe and what is important to me when making difficult decisions. As you develop your personal philosophy of mission, consider what you believe about health and its relationship to the gospel message; what you believe about the personhood of humans and their relationship to God; what you believe about nursing as a calling to ministry; and what you believe about creation and the environment and how we partner with God to care for it.

Some mission agencies focus on presenting the gospel and see health ministries as a way to convert people. Others are committed to helping the poor and underserved with quality health care and do not feel a need to present a gospel message to everyone who walks through the door. Still others are committed to a holistic ministry combining health care and the gospel message. Some see health as an avenue for community development. Find a sending organization with a mission philosophy that coincides with yours. Asking strategic questions related to philosophy will help you ascertain whether the written philosophy is congruent with how it is practiced on the field and with your personal philosophy of mission.

How you view human beings who are culturally different from yourself is important to a philosophy. I cringe when I hear people refer to others as *natives* or *heathen*. The person who uses such language communicates that others are inferior to themselves. Some cultural practices may seem primitive or based in demonic bondage, but people are human beings created in God's image, created by God to be loved by him, and to love him in return. If God's grace had not placed me in my culture with its material blessings, and if God had not revealed his love for me through his faithful servants, I might be *the one* to whom they are referring. God calls us to be his hands and feet in this world by loving others as he loved us. A well-developed philosophy of who we are, why we are here and our relationship with our Creator is foundational to a philosophy of mission.

Judith Shelly and Arlene Miller define nursing as "a ministry of compassionate care for the whole person, in response to God's grace toward a sinful world, which aims to foster optimum health *(shalom)* and bring comfort in suffering and death for anyone in need."[14] A philosophy of mission for missionary nurses needs to address how they view the nursing profession. Nursing is ministry and, as such, it is a call that God places on our lives. This gives confidence that in addition to the knowledge and skills we have gained from academic rigor and clinical practice, God has gifted us to do our work.

Finally, we must be aware of our environment. God has given us the resources of this earth to care for and to use in the building of his kingdom. He expects us to be good stewards of these resources. As missionary nurses, we need to be concerned about the air we breathe, the water we drink, the food we eat and the energy we use. We live in a *throw away* society that seeks instant gratification. Developing a philosophy for creation care and a lifestyle to support that belief will strengthen a philosophy of mission.

Going to grow

Mission experiences have much to teach us. First, we learn about God, the people and the world he has created and our partnership with him in building his kingdom. Second, we learn more about ourselves. As we move from the familiar to the unfamiliar, we expose some of our rough edges so God can work in our lives. Third, we grow professionally. As we care for people in a cross-cultural context, we can learn more about the God who heals and our dependence on him for guidance. We also grow in appreciation for colleagues in another country. We learn more about our inter-dependence and the teamwork it takes to provide health care in a mission context. Finally, we realize that being a missionary is not so much about what we are doing for God and others as what God and others have done for us.

Suggested Activities:

1. Write your philosophy of mission.
   - What do you believe about the relationship between health care and the gospel of Jesus Christ?
   - What do you believe about the people you are going to serve?
   - How do you view missionary nursing?
   - What is the Christian's responsibility in caring for creation?

2. Make a list of questions to ask a sending mission agency.

---

14 Judith Allen Shelly and Arlene B. Miller, *Called to Care: A Christian Theology of Nursing*, Downers Grove, IL: InterVarsity Press, 1999, p. 212.

RESOURCE MATERIALS

QUESTIONNAIRE[1]

Determine to what extent each of the following statements describes your thinking and approach to life. If the statement is not at all descriptive of you, write the number 1 in the blank space. If it is very descriptive of you, write the number 7. Write the number 4 if the statement describes you only somewhat. Use the number 2 or 3 for items that are less descriptive of you, and the number 5 or 6 for those that are more descriptive. Respond to all statements with a number from 1 to 7.

_____ 1. I would not feel comfortable working for a large company because I would never see the whole picture of what I was working on.

_____ 2. I seek out friends and enjoy talking about any subject that happens to come up.

_____ 3. I avoid setting goals for fear that I might not reach them.

_____ 4. I am more concerned about what I have accomplished than I am with the position and title of my job.

_____ 5. I seldom think much about the future; I just like to get involved in things as they turn up.

_____ 6. I feel things are either right or wrong; discussion of "gray" areas makes me uncomfortable and seems to compromise the truth.

_____ 7. When making a decision I feel that more than one of the options can be a right choice.

_____ 8. When I set a goal, I dedicate myself to reaching that goal, even if other areas of my life suffer as a result of it.

_____ 9. I am always one of the first to try something new.

_____ 10. I tend to associate only with people of the same social status.

_____ 11. I feel strongly that time is a scarce commodity, and I value it highly.

12. When my car needs tuning, I go to the dealer rather than let my neighbor who works out of his garage do the job. With professionals I know it will be done right.

13. I like performing before an audience because it pushes me to perform better.

14. My primary criteria for buying a car are low price and a record of quality and reliability; I do not let family or friends influence me to spend more for a "name brand."

15. My desk or work area is very organized. There is a place for everything, and everything is in its place.

16. I attend lectures and read books by experts to find solutions to issues of importance to me.

17. If offered a promotion which entailed moving to another city, I would not be held back by relationship to parents and friends.

18. I find it difficult to relate to people who have a significantly higher occupational or social position than mine.

19. I always wear a watch and refer to it regularly in order not to be late for anything.

20. I feel very frustrated if someone treats me like a stereotype.

21. I tend not to worry about potential problems; I wait until a problem develops before taking action.

22. When waiting in line, I tend to start up conversations with people I do not know.

23. I hate to arrive late; sometimes I stay away rather than walk in late.

24. I get annoyed at people who want to stop discussion and push the group to make a decision, especially when everybody has not had a chance to express their opinions.

25. I plan my daily and weekly activities. I am annoyed when my schedule or routine gets interrupted.

26. I do not take sides in a discussion until I have heard all of the arguments.

_____ 27. Completing a task is almost an obsession with me, and I cannot be content until I am finished.

_____ 28. I enjoy breaking out of my routine and doing something totally different every now and then to keep life exciting.

_____ 29. When involved in a project, I tend to work on it until completion, even if that means being late on other things.

_____ 30. I only eat in a few select public places outside of my home, where I can be sure the food is the best quality and I can find the specific items I enjoy.

_____ 31. Even though I know it might rain, I would attend a friend's barbecue rather than excuse myself to repair the damage a storm has done to my roof.

_____ 32. I always submit to the authority of my boss, pastor and teachers, even if I feel they may be wrong.

_____ 33. I feel that there is a standard English grammar and that all Americans should use it.

_____ 34. To make meals more interesting, I introduce changes into the recipes I find in cookbooks.

_____ 35. I argue my point to the end, even if I know I am wrong.

_____ 36. I do not feel that anything I have done in the past matters much; I have to keep proving my self every day.

_____ 37. When starting a new job, I work especially hard to prove myself to my fellow workers.

_____ 38. When introducing important people, I usually include their occupation and title.

_____ 39. I talk with others about my problems and ask them for advice.

_____ 40. I avoid participating in games at which I am not very good.

_____ 41. Even if in a hurry while running errands, I will stop to talk with a friend.

_____ 42. I have set specific goals for what I want to accomplish in the next year and the next five years.

_____ 43. I like to be active with many things so that at any one time I have a choice of what to do.

_____ 44. When shopping for a major item, I first get expert advice and then buy the recommended item at the nearest reasonable store.

_____ 45. I enjoy looking at art and trying to figure out what the artist was thinking and trying to communicate.

_____ 46. I feel uncomfortable and frustrated when a discussion ends without a clear resolution of the issue; nobody wins the argument.

_____ 47. I resist a scheduled life, preferring to do things on the spur of the moment.

_____ 48. When leading a meeting I make sure that it begins and ends on time.

[1] Sherwood G. Lingenfelter and Marvin K. Mayer, *Ministering Cross-Culturally: An Incarnational Model for Personal Relationships.* Grand Rapids, MI: Baker Books, a division of Baker Book House Company. 1986 (used with permission). This questionnaire may be (1) purchased separately in sets of 10, ISBN: 0-8010-5652-7, or (2) photocopied for classroom use without prior permission if $1.00 per copy is sent, with explanation to Baker Book House, P.O. Box 6287, Grand Rapids, MI, 49516-6287.

ANALYSIS

To determine your personal profile, fill in below your responses
to each of the corresponding statements in the questionnaire.
(If, for example, your response to statement 1 was 5, enter 5 in the
first space after "Holistic thinking.") Then add the five numbers in
each line and divide the total by five to obtain your average score
for each trait.

						Total	Avg
1. Time orientation	11	19	23	25	48		
2. Event orientation	5	24	29	31	47		
3. Dichotomistic thinking	6	10	15	33	46		
4. Holistic thinking	1	7	20	26	45		
5. Crisis orientation	6	12	16	30	44		
6. Noncrisis orientation	7	9	21	34	43		
7. Task orientation	8	12	17	27	42		
8. Person orientation	2	39	22	31	41		
9. Status focus	10	18	32	33	38		
10. Achievement focus	4	14	20	36	37		
11. Concealment of vulnerability	3	23	32	35	40		
12. Willingness to expose vulnerability	9	13	28	34	39		

PERSONAL PROFILE

On page 82, find on each axis your average score for that orientation. Then plot on each grid the point where the two average scores intersect. This point indicates your basic tendency.

The personal profile of basic traits is an approximate representation of the motivations behind the individual's actions within his or her culture. It will prove useful to compare the individual's profile with that of others. The matrix form presents the contrasting traits as concurrent forces pulling in different (but not necessarily opposite) directions. The scores on each matrix indicate the relative strength of each particular trait as one makes decisions and interacts with others. A score of (2,6) on the first grid (i.e., event has a priority rating of 2, a time rating of 6) suggests that the constraints of time exert a far stronger pull on the decisions and actions of the individual than does the commitment to completion of the events in which one participates. A score of (2,2) probably means that neither trait is exerting a strong influence.

The personal profile of basic values can be applied in several ways: (1) it can serve as the basis of a judgment against a person who does not behave as we would wish; (2) it can serve as a radar signal that we are headed for conflict with another person and thus should avoid confrontation; (3) it can serve as an insight which will help us achieve maximum intelligent interaction with another person. In *Caring Across Cultures* we see that by carefully choosing our responses to people and cultures whose orientations differ from ours, we can reduce or even resolve tensions in interpersonal relations.

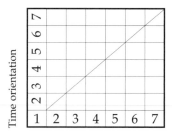

Event Orientation

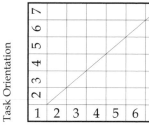

Person Orientation

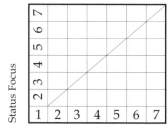

Achievement Focus

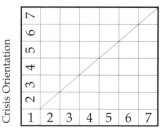

Noncrisis Orientation

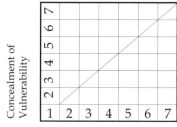

Willingness to expose vulnerability

APPENDIX A
RESOURCES FOR MISSIONARY NURSING
Medical Supplies, Equipment and Pharmaceuticals

MAP International   *MAP International has for many*
P.O. Box 215000   *years supplied pharmaceuticals*
Brunswick, GA 31521-5000   *and medical equipment. They also*
(912) 265-6010   *conduct workshops and maintain*
Fax: (912) 265-6170   *a supply of books and helpful*
www.map.org   *educational material.*

International Aid Inc.   *International Aid has a large*
17011 W. Hickory   *warehouse that refurbishes medical*
Spring Lake, MI 49456   *equipment and supplies gleaned*
(616) 846-7490   *from hospitals and offices that are*
Fax: (616) 846-3842   *upgrading. They will check electrical*
                                equipment and refit it for use in the

country to which you are sending it. They also assist missionaries with personal supplies and shipping. They have a limited supply of pharmaceuticals.

IDA   *International Dispensary Association*
P.O. Box 3098   *supplies mission hospitals and clinics*
1003 AB Amsterdam   *with pharmaceuticals in bulk at a*
The Netherlands   *reasonable cost. Their North*
(+31) 2903-3051   *American distributor is:*
(+31) 2903-1854 Fax   *World Response.*
Telex 1 35 66 ida nl

World Response
P.O. Box 684
Rollinsford, NH 03869
(603) 740-4664
(603) 474-4616 Fax
E-mail: Info@worldresponse.org

INMED
45449 Servern Way, Suite 161
Sterling, VA 20166
(703) 444-4477
(703) 444-4471 Fax
E-mail: inmed@ix.netcom.com

INMED is a non-profit organization that supplies medical equipment and supplies, medicines and educational materials to enable disadvantaged people worldwide to improve the health of their families and communities.

Health Education Materials

World Neighbors
4127 NW 122 Street
Oklahoma City, OK 73120-8869
(405) 752-9700

You can request their training materials catalog.

Teaching Aids at Low Cost (TALC)
P.O. Box 49 St Albans
Herts, AL1 4AX, U.K.
0 727 53867
Fax: 0 727 46852

A service that will locate specific materials in various languages at your request.

APPENDIX B
INSTRUCTIONS FOR
CONTINUING NURSING EDUCATION CREDIT

Nurses Christian Fellowship® has approved the enclosed material
for 5 contact hours of continuing nursing education credit. Nurses
Christian Fellowship,® Madison, Wisconsin, is approved as a provider of continuing education in nursing by the Wisconsin Nurses
Association Continuing Education Approval Program Committee,
which is accredited as an approver of continuing education in nursing
by the American Nurses Credentialing Center's Commission on
Accreditation.

Nurses who wish to receive CNE credit for this course will need to
complete the following:

1. Read the enclosed materials. If you have questions or wish to
    dialogue with the author via e-mail, you may contact her at
    GJTaz@aol.com.

2. Take the *Caring Across Cultures* CNE Post-test.
    70% is a passing score for the test.

3. Complete the continuing nursing education home study
    enrollment form online or on page 94.

4. Return
    a. The completed home study enrollment form with your
        identifying information
    b. $25.00 for CNE credit
To:
Caring Across Cultures CNE
Nurses Christian Fellowship
P.O. Box 7895
Madison, WI   53707-7895

You will be notified of your score within six weeks. If you pass, you
will be sent a certificate for 5 contact hours of CNE credit.

If you fail, you may retake the test once for an additional $5.00 fee.

CARING ACROSS CULTURES
CNE Post-Test

Please circle the letter preceding the correct response (use the form on page 94 to record your answers).

1. Which statement best describes a missionary nurse?
    a. Has advanced education in crosscultural nursing.
    b. Is motivated by faith in God to care for others in a location different than one's country of origin.
    c. Travels to dangerous places to care for others.
    d. Can practice nursing with few resources.

2. Which of the following is a realistic expectation for missionary nurses?
    a. To be protected from harm because of their service to God.
    b. To be welcomed to practice nursing in any country in which they work.
    c. To have their relationship with God tested and grow.
    d. To have all their physical needs met.

3. Who is the best example of a missionary?
    a. The apostle Paul.
    b. The apostle Peter.
    c. Hudson Taylor.
    d. Jesus Christ.

4. Which of the following is the most effective means of evangelism?
    a. Telling others what God has done for you.
    b. Providing excellent medical care.
    c. Making sure the message is culturally appropriate.
    d. Having an adequate financial support base for missionary work.

5. Which of the following is/are important to be an
    effective missionary?
    a. Study the Bible.
    b. Know that God has called you to the work.
    c. Talk to God in prayer.
    d. All of the above.

6. Which of the following describes culture shock?
    a. Low blood pressure that occurs when moving to
        a culture that is different from one's culture of origin.
    b. The conflict a person experiences when living in a
        culture with a value orientation different from one's own.
    c. The admiration for the arts in primitive cultures.
    d. Finding pathogens growing on laboratory media.

7. Which is *not* a stage of culture shock?
    a. Euphoria.
    b. Irritability.
    c. Depression.
    d. Adaptation.

8. Which of the following statements exemplifies the tension
    about self-worth in crosscultural ministry?
    a. Everyone is capable of succeeding, if they
        only apply themselves.
    b. Time is money.
    c. I must save face.
    d. It will all work out in the end.

9. Which of the following is the opposite of being time-oriented?
    a. Rule oriented.
    b. Event oriented.
    c. People oriented.
    d. Crisis oriented.

10. Which of the following is a descriptor of holistic thinkers?
    a. They avoid risks at all costs.
    b. They present three-point sermons.
    c. They need to understand the issue in its entirety before deciding.
    d. They value task over goal.

11. In which type of culture might people who confront conflict directly experience difficulty?
    a. In cultures where people are not afraid to fail.
    b. In cultures where failure is to be avoided at all costs.
    c. In cultures that encourage learning through failure.
    d. In cultures where it's okay to be careless.

12. Lingenfelter and Mayers advocate which of the following when attempting to resolve the tensions that occur when ministering cross-culturally?
    a. Changing your cultural style.
    b. Understanding where you fall on the assessment scale.
    c. Valuing the differences that cause the tension.
    d. Referring to Jesus as the model for crosscultural ministry.

13. Which of the following guidelines applies to an advanced practice nurse who will be practicing in mission settings?
    a. Study the protocols for the common illnesses in the host country.
    b. Be prepared to do major surgery.
    c. Critically evaluate the practice of the national nurses.
    d. Practice nursing only in remote areas where there is no access to health care.

14. Which of the following statements does *not* reflect
    Christian nursing in a mission setting?
    a. Use only pharmaceuticals whose expiration dates
        have not expired.
    b. Share your knowledge with the national nurses.
    c. Learn about the culture from national colleagues.
    d. It's not necessary to seek licensure in the host country.

15. Which of the following is descriptive of nurses in a
    mission hospital setting?
    a. They need to be demanding of their national staffs.
    b. They should have good management skills.
    c. They need to be able to focus only on the task at hand.
    d. They should be available 24 hours a day, 7 days a week.

16. Which of the following describes mission hospitals?
    a. Their focus is on the care of the sick, injured and dying.
    b. They are usually involved in the development of the
        communities that they serve.
    c. They can be sustained financially through
        charges for services.
    d. All of the above.

17. Which of the following is defined as "Using health as a
    vehicle to assist communities to take responsibility for the
    health and development of their own communities"?
    a. Primary health care.
    b. Community located health care.
    c. Community based health care.
    d. Community health development.

18. Which of the following methods is best for teaching village health workers?
    a. Lecture.
    b. Required reading.
    c. Non-formal education methods.
    d. Rote memorization.

19. What is the leading cause of death among missionaries?
    a. Malaria.
    b. Road accidents.
    c. Diarrhea from eating unwashed vegetables.
    d. HIV/AIDS.

20. Which of the following guidelines applies to using an interpreter?
    a. Speak rapidly so as not to waste valuable time.
    b. Use everyday speech, including idioms and clichés.
    c. Allow more time for the translation process.
    d. Ignore any suggestions from the translator regarding cultural context.

21. Which of the following statements best represents the work of missions?
    a. We are privileged to partner with God in his work of bringing others to have a personal relationship with him.
    b. We must share about Jesus with everyone we meet so that they don't go to hell.
    c. We do the best we can with what we have.
    d. We must sacrifice everything for the sake of bringing the message of Jesus Christ to those who do not know about him.

22. Which of the following is the best way to present the message of Jesus Christ within the context of a culture?
    a. We don't have to be concerned about the culture because the message of Jesus Christ transcends culture.
    b. As missionaries we shouldn't interfere with a culture when doing our work.
    c. We should learn as much about the culture and assume the position of a learner when approaching the culture.
    d. We need to identify the differences between our cultures and set about to change those areas so that the people can accurately understand the message of Jesus Christ.

23. What is the best order of events?
    a. Crisis, prayer, implementation.
    b. Plan, prayer, implementation.
    c. Crisis, implementation, prayer.
    d. Prayer, plan, implementation.

24. Asking the question "What was my expectation?" helps to address which of the following feelings?
    a. Frustration.
    b. Elation.
    c. Depression.
    d. Anxiety

25. Because malaria is so prevalent in tropical developing countries, the nurse can do which of the following when a patient presents with malarial symptoms?
    a. Treat all fevers as though the patient has malaria and move on to the next patient.
    b. Take a good history, obtain a malarial smear from the laboratory, and treat under the approved protocol.

c. Assume that people living in the tropics have immunity to malaria and investigate other potential diagnoses.

d. Instruct the patient to get some chloroquin tablets from the market and to take them until the patient feels better.

Caring Across Cultures
CNE Post-test is available online at:
www.ncf-jcn.org/ncfpress/cactest.html

CARING ACROSS CULTURES CNE Home Study Enrollment Form

Caring Across Cultures   Fee $25

Check One: ☐ RN   ☐ LPN   ☐ Other

Last Name _____ First _____ Mi _____ Phone _____

Address _____ City _____ State _____ Zip _____

State where licensed _____ **License#** _____

Pos/Title _____ Specialty Area _____

Test Responses: Circle the correct letter for your answer to each question.

1. A B C D	6. A B C D	11. A B C D	16. A B C D	21. A B C D
2. A B C D	7. A B C D	12. A B C D	17. A B C D	22. A B C D
3. A B C D	8. A B C D	13. A B C D	18. A B C D	23. A B C D
4. A B C D	9. A B C D	14. A B C D	19. A B C D	24. A B C D
5. A B C D	10. A B C D	15. A B C D	20. A B C D	25. A B C D

Photocopy and mail this card   Return to:
with a check for $25 made out   Caring Across Cultures CNE
to *Nurses Christian Fellowship*   Nurses Christian Fellowship
and **a self-addressed stamped**   P.O. Box 7895
business-size envelope.   Madison, WI 53707-7895

CNE
NCF PRESS
continuing education

Bibliography

Christine Aroney-Sine, *Survival of the Fittest.* 121 East Huntington
     Drive, Monrovia, CA: MARC, 1994.

Paul Borthwick, *Missions: God's Heart for the World.* Downers
     Grove, IL: InterVarsity Press, 2000.

Nancy J. Crigger and Lygia Holcomb, Beyond Band-Aids:
     Empowering a Honduran Community to Care.
     Journal of Christian Nursing, 17, no.1, Winter 2000, :30-35.

Daniel E. Fountain, *Primary Diagnosis & Treatment.* P.O. Box 50
     Brunswick, GA: MAP International, 1992.

Terri Goodman, Transcultural Nursing:
     A Personal and Professional Challenge.
     Nursing Clinics of North America, 19, no.1 :809-15.

Peter Jordon, *Reentry: Making the Transition from Missions to
     Life at Home.* P.O. Box 55787, Seattle, WA:
     YWAM Publishing, 1992.

Sherwood G. Lingenfelter and Marvin K. Mayers,
     *Ministering CrossCulturally: An Incarnational Model for
     Personal Relationships.* Grand Rapids, MI:
     Baker Book House, 1986.

Ruth A. Pakieser and Mary McNamee, How to Work with an
        Interpreter. *The Journal of Continuing Education in Nursing*,
        30, no.2, March/April 1999, :71-74.

Bonnie Petersen, Surviving Culture Shock:
        Lessons Learned as a Medical Missionary in Jamaica.
        Journal of Emergency Nursing, 21, 1995; :505.

J. Mack Stiles and Leeann. *Short-Term Missions*. Downers Grove, IL:
        InterVarsity Press, 2000. p. 62.

Judith Allen Shelly and Arlene B. Miller, *Called to Care:*
        A Christian Theology of Nursing. Downers Grove, IL:
        InterVarsity Press, 1999, p.212.

David Werner, *Where There is No Doctor.* P.O. Box 1692,
        Palo Alto, CA 94302: The Hesperian Foundation, 1977.

Catherine Wolf, and Dennis Palmer, *Handbook of Medicine in*
        Developing Countries, PO Box 7500, Bristol, TN:
        The Christian Medical & Dental Association, 1999.